The OddShoeFinder.com

Shoe Wearer's Handbook

Shoe Wearer's Handbook

How to:
- Get a good fit
- Choose the right shoes for the situation
- Avoid counterfeit designer and athletic shoes
- Care for your shoes
- Perform simple shoe repairs
- Find creative and productive uses for your old shoes

By
Clare Barron and Kent Basson

ISBN: 978-0-692-00803-4

Library of Congress Control Number: 2010922579

Table of Contents

Acknowledgments

SPECIAL THANKS TO CHRISTINA AND THE REST OF THE STAFF AT NEW to You boutique in Falls Church, Virginia, for allowing us to take photos in the store. Denise and Casey Reaves spent a lot of time taking photos and accumulating the subject matter of those photos. Christopher Quay and Gene Thompson did a great job on photographs and illustrations, respectively. Cathy Purdy, Marsha Pyanowski, and the editors at BookMasters were exceptionally patient with my limited knowledge of what is involved in publishing a book. Thanks to Ian Fieggen, who must know more about shoelaces than anyone else in history, for allowing us to use his diagrams of shoelacing methods. Finally, thanks to "My Twinhead" for pushing me to act on my ideas, and my sister Nancy for the inspiration for OddShoeFinder.com and for helping spread the word about the Web site.

    KB

    Special thanks to Tom Lehman, Eyad Houssami, and Eirini Kartsaki.

    CB

Introduction

PEOPLE IN INDUSTRIALIZED COUNTRIES ARE FORTUNATE TO HAVE AN incredibly wide range of footwear from which to choose. Zappos.com, a large online shoe retailer, carries about 500 brands of shoes. It is not uncommon for a brand to offer more than a hundred styles for each sex, with most styles available in multiple colors. Further, shoe styles change on a regular basis. Thus, there are probably hundreds of thousands of combinations of brands, styles, and colors of shoes available.

Every sport, occupation, and occasion has its own footwear. There are corrective and therapeutic shoes for many medical conditions. For $20 a pair, Wal-Mart offers shoes that would have been beyond the wildest dreams of most people just a few generations ago. At the other extreme, one can pay thousands of dollars for hand-crafted designer shoes.

The same economic forces that have given us such wide choices of affordable shoes have also driven up the value of labor in industrialized countries. As a result, many shoe stores have become little more than self-service warehouses with a clerk to ring up your sale after you have made your decision. Having a guide in the process of buying shoes to ensure proper fit and the appropriate shoes—although available at some upscale and specialty shoe stores—has become a luxury for which most are not willing to pay.

Until I was in my mid-thirties, I thought I had a medium-width foot. I also had a lot of trouble with foot pain. Until I went to a Red Wing shoe store in Bessemer, Alabama to buy work boots, I had no idea that I should have been wearing a narrow shoe. The owner and his employees were knowledgeable about what they were selling and realized the importance of a proper fit.

My experience at the Red Wing shoe store in Alabama led me to almost exclusively wear Red Wing shoes for about 10 years. I assumed that I would find similar expertise at all Red Wing shoe stores. I was disappointed when I moved and found that the owners of the local Red Wing store knew nothing about the shoe business. They had bought the store a few months earlier and could offer no help with my decision making.

If stores do not provide guidance in the shoe-buying process, we are largely on our own—with a bewildering array of choices. Some specialty shoes such as running shoes are reviewed in magazines. Retail shoe Web sites often have reviews written by those who have bought their shoes.

One problem with such buyer reviews is that satisfaction is highly influenced by expectations. Those who have been wearing cheaply made shoes will have very different expectations from those who splurge on their feet. Further, people who are disappointed with their purchases are probably more likely to write reviews. Thus, the reviews are of limited value.

While this book will never take the place of a knowledgeable salesperson, it is intended to give the layperson some guidelines for buying footwear and for getting the most out of footwear purchased.

CHAPTER 1
How to Get a Good Fit

Ever feel like one of Cinderella's stepsisters trying to cram your foot into an impossibly-shaped slipper? Luckily there is no need to chop off your toes or heel—à la the original Grimm fairytale—in order to make the shoe fit. But that does not mean that finding a shoe that properly fits your foot is easy! Not only do you have to search high and low for a quality product, you have to get to know your feet on a whole new level.

In this section, you will discover how to:

- determine your foot type
- measure your feet
- calculate shoe size
- convert American sizes into UK and European sizes
- identify the shoe's shank, vamp, and midsole

and much more! The skills you learn in this chapter will help you shop confidently the next time you decide to invest in a new pair of shoes. It is time to stop playing the part of the stepsister and embrace your inner Cinderella!

SHOPPING TIPS

Like it or not, you are the ultimate authority when it comes down to determining which pair of shoes fit your feet best. One brand may work miracles for your neighbor's feet but leave you limping.

Luckily, there are some basic principles that can help you in your quest to find a shoe that fits properly:

Buy shoes to fit your bigger foot.   It is better to wear shoes that are slightly loose than shoes that are too tight[1]. A loose shoe can be modified with special lacing techniques (see page 124), thick socks, or inserts. If your feet are more than one size apart from each other, consider investing in shoes that are two different sizes.

Shop during the afternoon or evening.   Most people's feet become slightly swollen by the end of the day. This is because gravity causes blood and other fluid to collect in the feet. Shopping when your feet are at their most swollen will ensure that you purchase shoes to fit your feet's maximum size.

Shop with socks, inserts, etc.   If you plan on wearing orthotics or inserts with your shoes, it is imperative to try on shoes with your inserts. They will drastically change the way the shoe fits. The same goes for shoes you intend to wear with thick socks or nylons.

---

1   It is prudent to follow Mr. Micawber's advice in *David Copperfield*: "Annual income twenty pounds, annual expenditure nineteen pounds nineteen and six, result happiness. Annual income twenty pounds, annual expenditure twenty pounds ought and six, result misery." With shoes: A little extra space, result happiness. Not quite enough space, result misery.

Leave ample space in the toe box. There should be 3/8 to 1/2 of an inch of space between your longest toe and the end of the shoe. Make sure that the toe box (the part of the shoe that contains the toes) is wide and deep enough for your toes to spread out comfortably.

GETTING TO KNOW YOUR FEET

When was the last time you thought seriously about your feet? How high are your arches? Would you consider your feet wide? Narrow? When was the last time you tried on a shoe in a different size?

It can be easy to forget about our feet. As long as they are not hurting us, there is no need to worry, right?

Actually, when it comes to the health of our feet, knees, hips, and back, there is much to be said for preventative care. One of the best ways to care for your feet is to wear supportive footwear that meets the specific needs of your feet. In order to know what kind of shoes to buy, you first have to get to know your feet.

- **Know your foot type.** Do you have high, low, or average arches? The answer to this question will determine the type of support you need inside your shoe. Turn to the next page for more information.

- **Know your size.** Did you know that the size of your foot changes over time? Turn to page 6 to learn how to accurately measure your foot.

- **Pay attention to width.** Shoe length is not the only important factor. A shoe that is too narrow or too wide can also spell

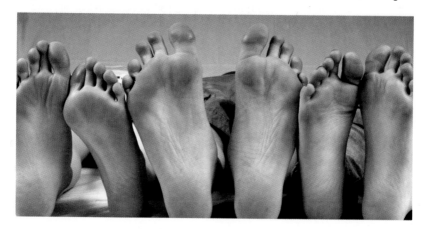

catastrophe for the health of your feet. Turn to page 7 to learn about determining the width of your feet.

DETERMINING YOUR FOOT TYPE

The shoes you wear can have a dramatic impact on the health of your feet, ankles, knees, hips, and back. In order to find footwear that properly supports your feet, it is important to identify whether you have high, average, or fallen arches.

The "wet footprint test" is one effective way of identifying your foot type. Simply dip your foot in water and place it on a brown paper bag or any other surface where your footprint will be visible.

Compare your footprint to the images below:

Fallen Arches

A person with fallen arches, or flat feet, will have an almost solid footprint with only a slight curve on the inside of the foot where the arch is located. People with this foot type tend to over-pronate. This means that their feet roll inward excessively with each step. Please turn to the next page to learn more about pronation.

Normal Arches

A person with normal arches will have a footprint with a moderate but noticeable arch. (You should see roughly half the width of your foot.) People with this foot type—the most common type of the three—enjoy the greatest flexibility when choosing shoes.

High Arches

A person with high arches will have a "scooped-out" footprint. The ball of the foot and heel will be connected by a thin line. People with high arches tend to be supinators, or under-pronators. This means that their feet do not roll sufficiently inward with each step. People with high arches generally require soft shoes with substantial arch supports and lots of cushioning. Please refer to page 48 for more information about shoes designed to accommodate under-pronation.

Note: The wet footprint test is an informal way of determining your foot type. Visit a salesperson at a quality shoe store or a podiatrist for an expert diagnosis. Wearing shoes that do not suit your foot type could lead to arch, heel, ankle or knee pain.

INTRODUCTION TO PRONATION

Imagine your foot as it rolls through its stride, transferring your body's weight from heel to toe. As the heel strikes the ground, the heel and ankle roll inward. This inward rotation is accompanied by the collapsing of the arch as the body's weight crosses the middle of the foot. Together these two motions make-up "pronation."

Pronation is a good thing! It is nature's way of providing the body with built-in shock absorption properties. However, some people's feet roll inward excessively when they walk or run. These people are classified as **over-pronators**. Other people have feet that do not roll inward enough. These people are classified as **under-pronators** or **supinators**.

Understanding the way your feet pronate is especially important when you are purchasing running or athletic shoes. Please turn to page 46 in the chapter "What to Look For in an Athletic Shoe" to learn more about pronation, over-pronation, and supination.

DETERMINING FOOT SIZE

Believe it or not, your foot changes size and shape over time. After years of bearing the body's weight, the arches gradually collapse and the foot gains length. People with high arches are particularly prone to increase in foot size as they age.

This change in size over time means that it is important to periodically measure your foot size. Just because you have been a size 7 for the last 10 years does not mean you will be a size 7 for the rest of your life.

For Accurate Results

Before you grab your measuring tape, please read the tips that follow:

- Measure your feet at the end of the day when your feet are the largest due to swelling.

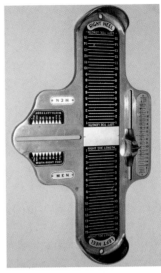

- Measure your feet wearing the socks you plan to wear with your new shoes, or without socks if you are planning to purchase sandals. (Unless you are one of those bold souls who rocks socks with your sandals.)

- Ask someone to measure your feet for you. The most accurate measurements are taken when you are standing with both feet firmly planted on the ground. Bending over to take a measurement distorts foot size and shape.

- Always measure both feet. It is rare to have two feet that are exactly the same size! This is true of both length and width.

- Use the larger measurement when determining your shoe size.

Note: If your feet are more than one size apart, you may need to purchase shoes that are different sizes. Please see page 16 to learn more about mismatched feet.

How to Measure Your Feet

In order to take an accurate measurement, you will need to measure tracings of your foot.

What You Need: Two pieces of paper, pen or pencil, ruler

What You Do:

- **Step 1.** Stand with each foot on a piece of paper. It is helpful to tape the paper to the ground.

- **Step 2.** Ask your friend to trace each foot with a pen or pencil. Make sure that the pen touches the foot at all times. Try to keep the pen as vertical as possible. If you do not have a friend to help you, measure your feet while sitting in a chair. This will produce more accurate results than standing.

- **Step 3.** Once you have finished measuring *both* feet, get out your handy ruler. It is time to measure the tracings!

  Foot Length: To calculate foot length, measure from the back of your heel to the tip of your big toe (i.e., the longest part of your foot). Subtract 1/5 inches to account for the distance of the pen from your foot.

  Foot Width: To calculate foot width, measure across the ball of your foot (i.e., the widest part of your foot). Subtract 1/5 inches to account for the distance of the pen from your foot.

- **Step 4.** Once you have calculated your foot length and foot width, look up these measurements on a standard shoe size chart.

You can find versions of Men's, Women's and Children's shoe size charts beginning on this page and page 11. If you would like to know how to calculate your shoe size yourself, please skip ahead to page 13.

Note: Be prepared to adjust your calculated shoe size based on the fit of a particular shoe. Not all brands are sized the same.

INTERNATIONAL SHOE SIZE CONVERSION CHARTS

WOMEN'S			
Inches	US	UK	EURO
8.17"	4	1.5	35
8.33"	4.5	2	35
8.5"	5	2.5	35 – 36
8.67"	5.5	3	36
8.83"	6	3.5	36 – 37
9"	6.5	4	37
9.17"	7	4.5	37 – 38

(Continued)

INTERNATIONAL SHOE SIZE CONVERSION CHARTS (*Continued*)

WOMEN'S			
Inches	US	UK	EURO
9.33"	7.5	5	38
9.5"	8	5.5	38 – 39
9.67"	8.5	6	39
9.83"	9	6.5	39 – 40
10"	9.5	7	40
10.17"	10	7.5	40 – 41
10.33"	10.5	8	41
10.5"	11	8.5	41 – 42
10.67"	11.5	9	42
10.83"	12	9.5	42 – 43

MEN'S			
Inches	US	UK	EURO
9.33"	6	5.5	39
9.5"	6.5	6	39
9.67"	7	6.5	40
9.83"	7.5	7	40 – 41
10"	8	7.5	41
10.17"	8.5	8	41 – 42
10.33"	9	8.5	42
10.5"	9.5	9	42 – 43
10.67"	10	9.5	43
10.83"	10.5	10	43 – 44
11"	11	10.5	44
11.17"	11.5	11	44 – 45
11.33"	12	11.5	45
11.67"	13	12.5	46
12"	14	13.5	47
12.33"	15		48
12.67"	16		49

(*Continued*)

INTERNATIONAL SHOE SIZE CONVERSION CHARTS (Continued)

CHILDREN'S			
Inches	**US**	**UK**	**EURO**
3.42"	0.5	0	16
3.58"	1	0.5	16
3.75"	1.5	1	17
3.92"	2	1	17
4.08"	2.5	1.5	18
4.25"	3	2	18
4.42"	3.5	2.5	19
4.58"	4	3	19
4.75"	4.5	3.5	20
4.92"	5	4	20
5.08"	5.5	4.5	21
5.25"	6	5	22
5.42"	6.5	5.5	22
5.58"	7	6	23
5.75"	7.5	6.5	23
5.92"	8	7	24
6.08"	8.5	7.5	25
6.25"	9	8	25
6.42"	9.5	8.5	26
6.58"	10	9	27
6.75"	10.5	9.5	27
6.92"	11	10	28
7.08"	11.5	10.5	29
7.25"	12	11	30
7.42"	12.5	11.5	30
7.58"	13	12	31
7.75"	13.5	12.5	31
7.92"	1	13	32
8.08"	1.5	14	33
8.25"	2	1	33

(Continued)

INTERNATIONAL SHOE SIZE CONVERSION CHARTS (*Continued*)

CHILDREN'S			
Inches	US	UK	EURO
8.42"	2.5	1.5	34
8.58"	3	2	34
8.75"	3.5	2.5	35
8.92"	4	3	36
9.08"	4.5	3.5	36
9.25"	5	4	37
9.42"	5.5	4.5	37
9.58"	6	5	38
9.75"	6.5	5.5	38
9.92"	7	6	39

Classifying Shoe Width

People tend to forget about shoe width when shopping for shoes, but it is just as important as determining an accurate shoe length. Cramming feet into shoes that are too narrow can lead to a host of common foot deformities and injuries such as bunions, hammertoe, corns, and calluses. Shoes that are too narrow also increase the likelihood of developing ingrown toenails and fungal toenail infections.

Shoes that are too wide are not able to hold the feet securely in place and subsequently fail to provide your feet with the support they need. Loose shoes can also lead to blisters, calluses, and other irritations caused by the shoe's rubbing against the foot.

Brands with Extra-Wide Sizes Available: ASICS, Avia, Bostonian, Croft & Barrow, Deer Stags, Dockers, Keds, Mootsies Tootsies, Natural-Soul, New Balance, Nike, Nunn Bush, Reebok and Skechers.

Brands with Narrow Sizes Available: Allen-Edmonds, Clarks, Mizuno, Munro, New Balance and Trotters.

Brands with a Spectrum of Widths: Brooks shoes offers widths that range from Narrow (2A) to Wide (2E). P.W. Minor also offers a wide range of widths, from Women's Narrow (2A) to Extra Wide (4E) and Men's Narrow (B) to Extra Wide (5E).

Note: New Balance and P.W. Minor make shoes of varying depths as well as widths.

SIZE STANDARD CHARTS FOR WIDTH

WOMEN'S			
Shoe	Width		
Size	Narrow	Average	Wide	X-Wide
5	2.81"	3.19"	3.56"	3.94"
5.5	2.88"	3.25"	3.63"	4"
6	2.94"	3.31"	3.69"	4.06"
6.5	3"	3.38"	3.75"	4.13"
7	3.06"	3.44"	3.81"	4.19"
7.5	3.13"	3.5"	3.88"	4.25"
8	3.19"	3.56"	3.94"	4.31"
8.5	3.25"	3.63"	4"	4.38"
9	3.31"	3.69"	4.06"	4.44"
9.5	3.38"	3.75"	4.13"	4.5"
10	3.44"	3.81"	4.19"	4.56"
10.5	3.5"	3.88"	4.25"	4.63"
11	3.56"	3.94"	4.31"	4.69"
11.5	3.63"	4"	4.38"	4.75"
12	3.69"	4.06"	4.44"	4.81"
12.5	3.75"	4.13"	4.5"	4.88"
13	3.81"	4.19"	4.56"	4.94"

(Continued)

SIZE STANDARD CHARTS FOR WIDTH (*Continued*)

Women's				
Shoe	Width			
Size	Narrow	Average	Wide	X-Wide
13.5	3.88"	4.25"	4.63"	5"
14	3.94"	4.31"	4.69"	5.06"
12.5	3.75"	4.13"	4.5"	4.88"
13	3.81"	4.19"	4.56"	4.94"
13.5	3.88"	4.25"	4.63"	5"
14	3.94"	4.31"	4.69"	5.06"

Note: Women's widths are most often described as narrow, medium, wide or extra wide. Sometimes they are expressed on an alphabetical scale that ranges from A at the narrowest to E at the widest.

Men's			
Shoe	Width		
Size	C	D	E
6	3.3"	3.5"	3.7"
6.5	3.3"	3.6"	3.8"
7	3.4"	3.6"	3.8"
7.5	3.4"	3.7"	3.9"
8	3.5"	3.8"	3.9"
8.5	3.6"	3.8"	4.0"
9	3.6"	3.9"	4.1"
9.5	3.7"	3.9"	4.1"
10	3.8"	4.0"	4.2"
10.5	3.8"	4.1"	4.3"
11	3.9"	4.1"	4.3"
11.5	3.9"	4.2"	4.4"
12	4.0"	4.3"	4.4"

(*Continued*)

SIZE STANDARD CHARTS FOR WIDTH (*Continued*)

MEN'S		
Shoe	**Width**	
Size	**C**	**D**	**E**
12.5	4.1"	4.3"	4.5"
13	4.1"	4.4"	4.6"
13.5	4.2"	4.4"	4.8"
14	4.2"	4.5"	4.9"
14.5	4.3"	4.6"	4.9"
15	4.3"	4.6"	5"

Note: Men's widths are traditionally scaled using letters so that C indicates a narrow fit and E indicates a wide fit. Sometimes B or A widths are also available for men.

Tips

When a number is placed in front of a letter, such as 2E, it amplifies the characteristics of that letter. For example, 4E is wider than 2E, and 4A is narrower than 2A. Sometimes instead of placing a number in front of the letter, shoe companies simply write the letter multiple times. Thus 4A is the same width as AAAA.

You will occasionally see the width marking "S" or "SS." This stands for "Slim" and is equivalent to a Narrow sizing.

Calculating Shoe Size

Whether you realize it or not, Americans measure their feet in barleycorns—the ancient Roman unit that equals 1/3 of an inch. The "barleycorn" represented the size of an average corn of barley. Edward II of Britain created a shoe sizing system based on the barleycorn in 1324, and we have been sizing our shoes in 1/3 inch units ever since.

King Edward's foot was 36 barleycorns long; at the time, this was graded a size 12. Today we use a different formula to calculate shoe size.

For Men:	$3 \times$ length of foot $- 22 =$ shoe size
For Women:	$3 \times$ length of foot $- 20.5^2 =$ shoe size
For Children:	$3 \times$ length of foot $- 9.75 =$ shoe size

It is helpful to examine the above formulae with an example. Let's imagine we are determining shoe size for a foot measurement that is 10 inches long. If the measurement belongs to a man, then the calculated shoe size would be 8. If the measurement belongs to a woman, then the calculated shoe size would be 9.5.

Man's Size:	$(3 \times 10) - 22 = 8$
Woman's Size:	$(3 \times 10) - 20.5 = 9.5$

The discrepancy between men's and women's sizes is the result of the constant.[3] Why the constant is different for men and women is a mystery. At least, no one is sure historically who made the call, or why it was im-

portant to distinguish between the sexes. You will note that children's sizes in the U.S. system are the same for both genders. Likewise, the European and UK systems do not have separate women's and men's sizes.

American System and International Conversions

The need for a uniform shoe sizing system arose during the Civil War when mass-produced left and right shoes were manufactured for the first time in order to provide soldiers with boots that fit. Twenty years later, Edwin B. Simpson revolutionized the mass production of shoes by developing a more detailed sizing system that included half sizes and varying widths. In Simpson's system, half sizes were 1/6 of an inch apart and

---

2 This number is sometimes listed as 20 and 21 in addition to 20.5.

3 A constant is any number in a mathematical equation that is independent of measurement. For example, 22 in the men's formula is a constant. It is always 22 no matter the length of the foot.

width was measured in 1/4-inch increments. This system was adopted by American and British shoe manufacturing companies in 1888.

 The UK System. The UK system is similar to the American one. Both measure full sizes in 1/3-inch increments. However, the UK system starts with size 0, while the US system starts with size 1. The result is that there is roughly 0.5 size difference between UK and U.S. men's shoes. For example, a U.S. men's size 8 would be approximately a UK men's size 7.5.

This is not true for women's sizes. Unlike UK sizes, American sizes differ with gender. Therefore there is a difference of 2.5 sizes between UK and U.S. women's shoes. For example, a U.S. women's size 8 would be approximately a UK women's size 5.5.

 The European System. The most commonly used European system is the Paris Point system. Each size is roughly 2/3 of a centimeter. Converting U.S. sizes into European sizes is complicated. You can do an approximate conversion by adding 30 to an American women's size and 32 to an American men's size.

Note: Turn to the next page for a convenient conversion chart.

Other Common Conversions

Athletic Shoes.   It is normally a good idea to purchase athletic shoes that are slightly bigger than your everyday shoes or dress shoes. This is because the foot swells during physical exercise. It is also important not to cram the foot into athletic shoes. This could lead to injuries such as ingrown or bruised toenails and infections such as athlete's foot and fungal toenail infections. Most people find that purchasing a pair of athletic shoes 1/2 size bigger than their normal size provides an appropriate fit.

Gender Conversions.   As mentioned on the previous page, men's and women's shoes are not sized the same in the American system. To convert from a women's size to a men's size, add 1.5 to 2 sizes to the women's size. To make a conversion in the opposite direction, you will need to subtract the same figure.

The charts below are intended as a quick reference for common shoe conversions. Note: These charts help you approximate the correct shoe size. Use the International Shoe Size Conversion Charts for more accurate conversions. Or better yet, try on the shoes in question.

WOMEN'S US	UK	Subtract 2.5
	EURO	Add 30
	Athletic	Add 0.5
	Men's US	Subtract 2

MEN'S US	UK	Subtract 0.5
	EURO	Add 32
	Athletic	Add 0.5
	Women's US	Add 2

MISMATCHED FEET

It is easy to look to the body as an example of perfect symmetry. Everything comes in twos—two eyes, two ears, two arms, two hands, two legs, two feet. We expect these "partners in crime" to work together in a way that makes life easier. Your left eye may not see 20:20, but perfect vision in your right eye can make the overall picture clearer. Different sized feet, unfortunately, make life more complicated. Not only do differences in foot size and shape make it difficult to purchase shoes, they also can throw your body's alignment out of whack.

When it comes to mismatched feet, it is important to care for each foot in turn. One foot should not have to suffer in order to make the other one more comfortable. Forcing a foot into a shoe that is too tight or too large, or one that does not provide the proper orthopedic support, will only lead to additional foot maladies. Unfortunately, shoes come in perfectly matched pairs (unlike our imperfectly matched feet). Purchasing *two pairs* of shoes in order to acquire *one pair* of shoes that meets the needs of your feet is a frustrating and expensive experience. And it is one familiar to all too many people. Some studies suggest that upwards of 60 percent of Americans have feet that are two different sizes.

Keep these simple rules in mind when shopping for shoes for mismatched feet:

- **Don't sweat the small stuff.** Few of us have feet that are identical in size. If your feet are only 1/2 size apart, or even a full size, you may be able to wear the same size shoe on each foot with a few minor adjustments.

- **Let the big dog lead.** You should always purchase shoes with your *larger* foot in mind. It is easier to tighten a slightly loose shoe using inserts or special shoe tying techniques (see page 124) than it is to make a too tight shoe stretch.

- **Shop around.** Although Nordstrom[4] is a notable exception, most department stores do not have easy solutions for people who need right and left shoes in different sizes. You may be forced to buy two pairs of shoes in order to have one pair that fits your mismatched feet. Instead, buy shoes from online retailers or specialty stores that will let you mix and match sizes. We may be a little partial, but you may want to check out OddShoeFinder.com, where users with mismatched feet can find mismatched shoes posted by others, post their own pairs of mismatched shoes (left over from buying one pair for the size of each foot), and even find their "sole" mates – users with complementary foot sizes.

ANATOMY OF A SHOE

In addition to knowing the ins and outs of your feet, it is important to understand the basic anatomy of a shoe. Whether a sports shoe is advertised with an EVA midsole, or a dress shoe is described as having a full leather upper, understanding the various parts of the shoe and why they are important will help you to become a confident consumer who makes smart choices when purchasing shoes.

---

4 Nordstrom department stores have long offered mismatched pairs of shoes for those with feet at least two sizes different from each other. The policy is attributed to the store founder's wife, a polio survivor.

Use the handy glossary to look up definitions of a shoe's major parts. Following the glossary, you will find pictures of shoes with the parts labeled.

Shoe Glossary

Aglet: The plastic casing on the end of a shoelace that makes it easier to pass through the eyelet.

Arch Support: Support for the arch of the foot. Arch support features are usually incorporated into a shoe's footbed or insole. The insole is

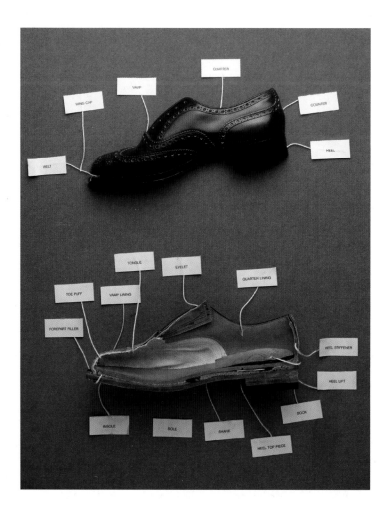

built-up so that a firm ridge lies immediately below the foot's arch. Arch supports can also be inserted separately into the shoe.

Back Seam: The vertical seam at the back of the shoe that runs from the bottom of the heel up to the Achilles tendon.

Collar: Material that is stitched to the rim of the shoe (see topline). Collars are often padded for comfort.

Eyelet: The hole that the lace passes through. Eyelets are usually rimmed with plastic, metal, cord, leather or some other material that makes it easy for the lace to pass through.

Feather: The part of the shoe where the upper meets the sole.

Footbed: The part of the shoe that runs along the bottom of the foot. When footbeds are designed to fit the natural curvature of the foot, they are often described as "contoured." Often referred to as the insole.

Foxing: A strip of rubber that joins the upper and sole of a shoe. Commonly found on canvas sneakers.

Goring: A small, triangular insert of stretchy material that joins two pieces of the upper. Gorings are often found on slip-on shoes that lack laces.

Heel: The part of the shoe that protects and sometimes elevates the heel of the foot.

Heel Breast: The part of the heel that faces forward when a shoe is worn.

Heel Counter: A rigid element (often made of plastic) usually concealed within the fabric of the shoe at the back of the heel. The heel counter cups the heel and provides extra support. To find out if a shoe has a heel counter, press your thumbs against the back of the heel. If the heel bends easily, there is no heel counter.

Heel Seat: The part of the sole where the heel seats.

Hook and Loop Fasteners: A type of fastener that uses two pieces of fabric, one piece which has "hooks" and the other which has finer "loops" that get caught in the hooks. Velcro® is a well-known brand of hook and loop fastener.

Inseam: A hidden seam that holds together the welt, upper, sole, and insole.

Insole: The part of the sole you see when you look inside your shoe. Insoles are often curved to provide arch support. They are also often removable.

Laces: A thin piece of material that is threaded through the eyelets. When tightened, laces secure the shoe on the foot.

Last: The form on which a shoe is constructed. Lasts can be straight, curved, or semi-curved; they determine the inside shape of the shoe.

Lug Sole: A rubber outsole with deep indentations that increase a shoe or boot's traction.

Midsole: The part of the sole concealed between the insole and the outer sole. Midsoles vary widely in weight, support, and flexibility. Technological advances related to cushioning, support, and flexibility are often located in this area of the shoe.

Outsole: The part of the sole that comes into contact with the ground.

Quarter: The part of the upper that covers the sides and rear of the heel. The quarter is located between the heel and the vamp.

Seat: The part of the insole that holds the heel in place.

Shank: A thin piece of metal or other rigid material that runs from the heel across the arch of the foot and provides shape to the shoe and support to the foot. The shank is concealed between the insole and the outer sole of the shoe.

Sipes: Thin channels made with a razor on a rubber sole. Sipes are designed to dispel water and prevent slipping. Although sipes are a familiar feature on most boat shoes, rumor has it that they were first invented for shoes worn in slaughterhouses.

Sock Liner or Lining: A thin piece of material that lies directly beneath the sole of the foot and is attached to the shoe's insole.

Sole: The combination of the insole, midsole, and outsole. Sometimes the term sole is used to refer to the outsole only.

Throat: The opening of the shoe where a foot enters.

Toe Box: The front part of the shoe that contains your toes. Toe boxes sometimes have toe caps that are stitched over the material of the upper. Toe caps can be decorative, or they can provide protection for the toes.

Tongue: A strip of material that sits on the top of your foot and is designed to protect your foot from rubbing against the shoe's laces.

Top Piece or Lift: The part of the heel that comes into contact with the ground. The top piece is usually made of a hard, durable material.

Topline: The upper edge of the shoe.

Tread: The grooves on the bottom of a rubber sole.

Upper: The part of the shoe that covers the top of the foot. Together, the upper and the entire sole (insole, midsole and outer sole) make up the basic building blocks of a shoe.

Vamp: The part of the upper that covers the front of the foot. The vamp usually contains the shoe's laces, buckle or whatever device is used to fasten the shoe.

Waist: The "skinny" area of the shoe near the arch or the in-step. Where the shoe curves inward.

Welt: A strip of material that covers and reinforces the area where the upper meets the sole (the feather).

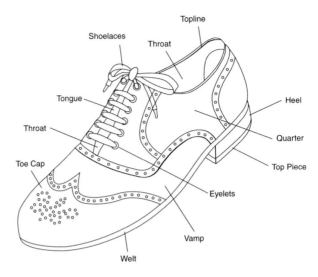

Figure 1. Diagram of a Dress Shoe

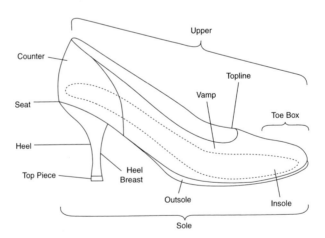

Figure 2. Diagram of a High Heel

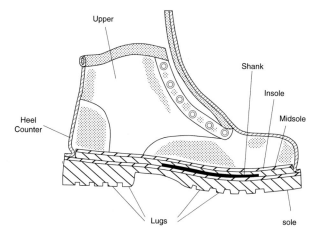

Figure 3. Cutaway of a Boot

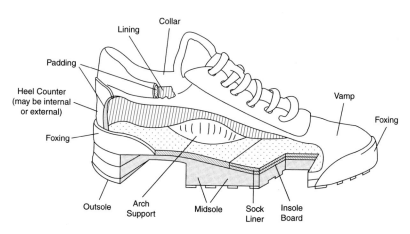

Figure 4. Cutaway of an Athletic Shoe

CHAPTER 2

What to Look for in Sandals, High Heels, and Dress Shoes

CERTAIN SHOE-FITTING PRINCIPLES CAN BE APPLIED TO JUST ABOUT ANY article of footwear: Does the shoe properly support your arch and cushion your heel? Is the toe box wide enough for your toes to lie comfortably flat? And most important, is the shoe comfortable?

But that is not to say that a boot should fit your foot like a high heel or a sandal should fit like an athletic shoe. (Unless you take after the Ancient Greeks and wear sandals when you throw the javelin!) Shoe fit is determined by shoe function, and different shoes are definitely designed with different goals in mind. You want a high heel that will make your legs look divine and a sandal that will be comfortable at the beach.

In this section, you will discover how to:

- find a sandal you can wear walking, running, or backpacking
- choose a high heel that does not hurt your feet
- pick out a high-quality leather dress shoe

and much more! Choosing your shoes with specific goals and fit-features in mind will lead to many happy years of use.

CHARACTERISTICS OF FOOT-FRIENDLY SANDALS

Just because it is summer does not mean you get to take a vacation from proper footwear! Sandals come in all sorts of designs that are fashionable *and* orthopedically smart.

Look for sandals with a:

✓ **Flexible Forefoot:** A flexible forefoot will help you to roll through your foot from heel to toe without altering your natural stride. Avoid sandals with rigid soles that cause the feet to "slap" the ground.

Note: A sandal with a flexible forefoot is not the same as a sandal with a soft, bendy sole. You are looking for a sandal with a gentle flex, not a sandal that you can bend in half. The sole should be firm enough to give your feet proper support.

✓ **Contoured Footbed:** Many sandals sport flat footbeds that offer little support. Look for sandals with contoured footbeds designed to complement the natural curves of the feet. Contoured footbeds usually include some kind of arch support, heel cup and toe grip.

✓ **Ankle Strap:** It does not matter if your sandal closes with a buckle or hook and loop fasteners such as Velcro®. What is important is that the shoe holds your foot securely in place. The foot should not travel back and forth in the footbed, and the heel should not slide up and down. Look for sandals with straps that encircle the ankle.

✓ **Cushioned Midsole:** Look for sandals that offer shock absorption features. Cushioning in the heel is particularly important as this is the part of the foot that bears the brunt of your weight.

THE PROBLEM WITH FLIP-FLOPS

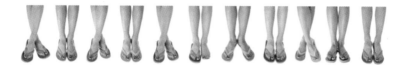

Forget the pool or the beach; you can spot flip-flops just about anywhere. Whether people are heading to a party or climbing into the shower, chances are someone's feet are adorned with these flexible thongs.

Without a doubt, flip-flops have some excellent selling points: They are comfortable, cheap and easy to slip on and off. They keep your feet cool *and* they come in every color imaginable.

Unfortunately, flip-flops do your feet no favors in the long run. A recent study conducted at Auburn University revealed that wearing flip-flops for extended periods of time can seriously harm the health of your feet, ankles, hips, and lower back. A team of researchers videotaped 39 volunteers wearing flip-flops and then wearing traditional athletic shoes. The study revealed that wearing flip-flops had negative consequences on a person's gait. Study participants tended to grip the footbed with their toes in an effort to keep the flip-flops on their feet. This motion not only leads to sore and stressed toes, it also negatively affects the plantar fascia—the connective tissue that runs along the bottom of the arch. Flip-flop wearers also tend to take shorter steps and land with less force on their heels. This means that the rest of the foot has to work harder in order to make up for the heel, which usually absorbs the majority of the impact each time the foot strikes the ground.

The study does not suggest that we should give up flip-flops altogether. Instead, the message is one of moderation. Flip-flops were designed to be worn between the locker-room and the pool. They are not meant to be worn all day, every day for months at a time. If you are a habitual flip-flop wearer, consider alternating between flip-flops and supportive sneakers. Or try wearing flip-flops no longer than 5 hours at a time. Flip-flops should also be discarded every 3 to 4 months. Like athletic shoes, they lose their ability to cushion your feet over time.

SPECIALTY SANDALS

Have you ever considered hiking in a sandal? What about playing soccer? Or going for an 8-mile run? Specialty sandals are all about taking the sandal anywhere a closed-toe shoe can go.

Walking Sandals

Walking sandals are designed to be worn on short- and long-distance walks. They are heavier and more durable than regular sandals and should provide excellent traction and cushioning.

Look for walking sandals with:

- **Sturdy, Adjustable Straps.** The sandal should fasten securely to your feet so that your heel does not slide up and down and your foot does not slide forward and back in the footbed.
- **Toe Guards.** An optional feature, the toe guard is designed to keep grit and dirt out of your shoes and to prevent you from stubbing your toe.

Walking sandals sometimes come with fit-features similar to running and walking shoes. You can find walking sandals with motion control, stability, and cushioning features.

Be sure to choose a sandal designed for your specific physical activity.

Trail Sandals

Trail sandals are made to be used on natural trails and backpacking trips.

Look for sandals with:

- padded straps to prevent irritation and blisters
- anti-pronation midsole plugs (if motion control is necessary)
- excellent traction features on the outsole

Tips

Choose sandals that are lightweight. You will have to carry them in your pack! Also, avoid leather sandals; they tend to not hold up well on the trail.

Casual Walking Sandals

Casual walking sandals are made for casual in-city walkers.

Look for sandals with:

- cushioned heels and arch support

- padded straps to prevent irritation and blisters

- waterproof material to keep feet dry

Tips

Leather sandals are an excellent choice for casual walking sandals, but make sure the leather is waterproof.

Athletic Sandals

Athletic sandals are designed to support and protect the foot during rigorous athletic activity. Some people prefer athletic sandals over athletic shoes because the sandals are lightweight and keep feet cool thanks to increased air circulation.

Like walking sandals, athletic sandals should sport adjustable straps for a snug fit. A toe guard or covered toe is particularly recommended for people who plan to exercise outdoors.

Running Sandals

Running sandals are made for long-distance running and field sports.

Look for sandals with:

- adjustable straps for a secure fit

- midsole cushioning

- anti-pronation midsole plugs

- excellent traction

- flexible forefoot

- mesh upper to promote air circulation
- quick-drying nylon straps

Tips

Look for running sandals that match your foot type. If you plan to run outside, or wear your sandals while playing team sports, be sure to choose sandals with a covered toe or toe guard.

Water-Sport Sandals

Water sport sandals are made for waterskiing and other water sports.

Look for sandals with:

- quick-drying nylon straps
- cleated or lugged rubber outsoles
- toe guards
- drainage ports

THE PROBLEM WITH HIGH HEELS

Here are some figures for you: Approximately 3.5 billion dollars are spent each year in the United States for women's foot surgeries. On top of that enormous cost, the female workforce misses 15 million workdays each year because of foot injuries and surgeries. Unfortunately, a great deal of these foot  problems are self-inflicted, and one of the biggest culprits is the high heel shoe.

It is no secret that high heels hurt your feet. Ask any woman who has spent the night teetering in 4-inch stilettos. But what some women may not realize is the extent to which wearing high heels contributes to long-term health consequences such as osteoarthritis and bunions. Unlike sore feet, these foot conditions do not go away overnight.

- **Bad Posture.** High heels shift your center of gravity forward so that your hips and spine are pushed out of alignment.

- **Knee Pain and Osteoarthritis.** Altered posture caused by wearing high heels leads to increased pressure on the inside of the knee. Repeated stress in this area dramatically increases the chances of developing osteoarthritis.

- **Shortening of the Achilles Tendon.** The elevation of the heel causes the Achilles tendon to shorten over time. A short, tight Achilles tendon increases the risk of injuries such as Achilles tendinitis and plantar fasciitis.

- **Smaller Calf Muscles.** The elevation of the heel also causes the calf muscles to contract. If high heels are worn consistently, calf muscles can become short and weak, which promotes injury.

- **Foot Injuries and Deformities.** The combination of cramped toe boxes and the downward angle of the high heel can cause and/or aggravate foot deformities and injuries including bunions, hammertoe, Morton's neuroma, plantar fasciitis and Achilles tendinitis.

CHARACTERISTICS OF FOOT-FRIENDLY HIGH HEELS

Although high heels do your feet no favors, few women are willing to give up their kitten heels or 4-inch stilettos without a fight. If you *must* have your heels, then consider choosing high-heeled shoes that will reduce your risk of developing an injury or deformity.

✓ **Rubber sole.** Although a leather sole is usually a sign of quality and high-fashion, rubber soles are actually kinder to your body when it comes to high-heeled shoes. A rubber sole offers extra flexibility and increases your grip on the floor.

✓ **Solid heel.** Itty-bitty heels increase pressure on the balls of your feet. By choosing a shoe with a wider heel, you can distribute weight more evenly between the heel and forefoot. But be warned: While wider heels are better for your feet, they do little to alleviate stress on your knees.

✓ **Two inches or less.** Limit yourself to heels that are 2 inches or shorter. These shoes will give you enough lift to show off your legs *and* reduce the risk of foot injuries and/or deformities.

Tip

Platform heels give the illusion of a higher heel height.

✓ **Round or square toe.** High heel styles that allow your toes to lay flat comfortably are a worthwhile investment. Pointy-nosed shoes that cramp your toes can lead to deformities such as hammertoe, bunions, corns, and Morton's neuroma. If you value the health of your feet, then square-toed shoes are always in style! Or better yet, opt for an open-toed shoe.

✓ **Cushioned ride.** High-heeled shoes come with cushioning and arch support too! Nike has even released a line of heels that incorporates its "Air Sole" technology. With a cushion of air under the ball of the foot and heel, the foot, ankle, and knees benefit from excellent shock absorption and support.

✓ **Rule of thumb.** Purchase high heels that have a thumbs-width of space from the big toe to the end of the shoe when you are *standing*.

TIPS FOR ENJOYING YOUR HEELS WITHOUT INJURY

Tip #1: Break in your heels instead of breaking your feet.

There is no need to suffer through blisters and calluses for a new pair of heels. The "break-in" process should be virtually pain free. Turn to page 113 to learn about painless ways to soften a pair of stubborn heels.

Tip #2: Price matters.

When it comes to shoes, price is often a good indicator of quality. It is worth spending more money on one pair of quality, versatile heels than snapping up several cheap pairs. Remember: High heels can have orthopedic features such as a pillowed heel and cushioned midsole.

Tip #3: Walk the plank.

Always test out new shoes on hardwood floors. Trying out high heels on carpet will give you a false sense of cushioning.

Tip #4: Like most fine things in life, high heels are best enjoyed in moderation.

Avoid wearing high heels all day (or all night)! These shoes will do less damage if you only wear them for a few hours at a time. Pack a light pair of flats in your purse so you can change out of your heels as soon as they become uncomfortable.

Tip #5: Who says being fashionable is not a sport?

Stretch your calves before and after you wear high heels. This will lengthen the muscles (as well as the Achilles tendon) and could help prevent injury.

CHARACTERISTICS OF HIGH-QUALITY DRESS SHOES

Leather is the name of the game when it comes to choosing high-quality dress shoes for men and women. These shoes may cost a pretty penny, but they will last through the years. In fact, many people find it less expensive to refurbish the same pair of high-quality dress shoes than to replace lower-quality shoes on a regular basis.

For high quality dress shoes, look for shoes with:

✓ **Leather Uppers:** The uppers of your dress shoe should be made from a high-quality leather such as napa or calfskin. It is also common for shoes to be made from full grain side leather, which is a slightly less expensive option. Women's dress shoes are sometimes made from kidskin, which comes from young goats, and exotic leathers such as alligator or ostrich are also popular.

Inspect the leather for blemishes; a high quality shoe should not have visible scars or other markings on the leather.

For more information on how to care for leather shoes, please turn to page 106.

✓ **Leather Soles:** Some people aesthetically prefer leather soles over rubber ones. Others claim they are cooler in the summer, or more comfortable for indoor-wear. Whatever the reason, leather soles have become one of the hallmarks of a high quality dress shoe.

✓ **Leather Insoles:** Insoles should be made from leather and not from layers of cardboard or other synthetic material.

✓ **Leather Lining:** High-quality dress shoes will sport a leather lining. Check to make sure that the lining is stitched together discreetly with smooth, sturdy seams.

✓ **Sturdy, Discreet Stitching:** Dress shoes should be stitched together, and the stitching should be barely noticeable. In particular, check to make sure that the sole is stitched to the body of the shoe and not glued.

FOOT-FRIENDLY DRESS SHOES

Often high-quality dress shoes are orthopedically friendly for your feet. There are some exceptions, however. Leather soles may be aesthetically pleasing, but rubber soles provide better traction and cushioning. Foot-friendly features such as spacious toe boxes, low heel height, and breathable uppers are still important even when shopping for shoes that will be worn on a rare evening out.

For foot-friendly dress shoes, look for shoes with:

✓ **Breathable Uppers:** Most quality dress shoes are made from leather. The quality of leather varies; look for shoes made from full grain leather with few blemishes.

Leather shoes should allow air to flow through the shoe, keeping the foot dry and odor free. If you choose dress shoes made from synthetic materials, make sure that the material will not cause your feet to sweat.

✓ **Rubber Soles:** Rubber soles provide excellent traction and cushioning. They also hold up on wet, rainy days far better than leather soles, which can become treacherously slippery.

✓ **Spacious Toe Boxes:** Choose dress shoes that are wide and deep enough for your toes to comfortably spread out. You should have plenty of wiggle room without feeling like your foot is sliding around inside the shoe.

> **Note:** A well-fitted toe box is one of the most crucial features when it comes to preventing common foot deformities.

✓ **Smooth Lining:** A quality dress shoe should sport a smooth lining with clean seams and edges. Look for shoes that offer a seamless or "soft" fit; this will minimize irritation that can lead to blisters and calluses.

✓ **Low Heel:** Try to keep heel height between 1/2 and 2 inches.

GLOSSARY: SHOE TYPES AND STYLES

Antiquing: A leather finish designed to make shoes appear weathered. The effect is usually achieved with polish.

Athletic Shoe: Closed-toe, rubber-soled shoes designed to support the foot during physical exercise and enhance athletic performance.

Ballerina Flat: A woman's flat inspired by the ballet slipper. Ballerina flats are low cut (i.e., they expose the upper part of the foot) and have a closed toe.

Balmorals: A type of Oxford shoe. Balmorals typically have no seams other than the toe cap. They are also distinguished by their "V" shaped lacing panel over the instep.

Bespoke: Hand-made shoes designed for a particular customer.

Blucher: A leather shoe that is made with two parallel flaps that are laced together across the forefoot. Blucher shoes are easier to adjust than balmorals.

Boat Shoes: A casual, closed-toe shoe designed to be worn on a boat. Boat shoes have a rubber-siped sole. (Sipes are narrow grooves in the sole of a shoe designed to dispel water in order to prevent slipping.)

Boot: A shoe with an upper that extends above the ankle.

Brogue: A heavy oxford-style shoe. Brogues usually have wingtips and brogueing or perforations. The shoes originally were popular country shoes in Scotland and made from untanned leather.

Brogueing: Ornamental designs along the seams of a shoe. Brogueing is done by punching holes in the upper. These holes were originally designed to allow water to drain easily.

Cap Toe: This shoe style is adorned with a toe cap that is roughly shaped like the letter "D." Men's dress shoes are commonly designed with a cap toe; some would also classify Converse® All Stars® as cap toe shoes.

Chukka Boot: An ankle-height boot. Chukka boots are lace-ups and have little ornamentation. They are usually made from calfskin or suede.

Clog: A shoe with a closed toe and open back. Clogs have a platform heel. They were originally made with wooden soles.

Derby: A man's leather dress shoe. Derby shoes are distinguished by their open style of lacing that increases the shoe's adjustability. The tongue and vamp of a Derby shoe are made from the same piece of leather. But instead of a "V" shaped lacing panel, the vamp is split into two parallel flaps (| |) that are laced together. *See blucher.*

Embossed Leather: Any leather to which a pattern has been applied by extreme pressure. Sometimes embossed leather is used to imitate specialty leathers such as crocodile.

Espadrille: A shoe or sandal with woven rope covering the sole. The upper is usually canvas. Espadrilles are popular summer shoes.

Flat: A woman's shoe with little to no heel.

French binding: A thin strip of cloth or other material that is sewed along the shoe's uppermost edge (i.e., its topline) and folded over.

Jelly Shoes: Shoes made entirely of Polyvinyl Chloride—a translucent, rubbery material. Also spelled Jellie.

Jodhpur Boot: A low-cut boot originally designed for horseback riding.

Loafer: A slip-on shoe with no laces, buckles or any other fasteners. Loafers originated in Norway and should provide a soft, comfy fit.

Mary Jane: A woman's closed-toe shoe characterized by a strap across the instep. Mary Janes can come with low-to-medium heel height.

Medallion: An ornamental design on the toe cap of a men's or women's dress shoe. A Medallion is usually made by punching small holes in the upper.

Moccasins: A soft, leather slipper. Moccasins are traditionally made with a single piece of leather for the bottom, side and back parts of the shoe. The vamp is attached to the rest of the shoe with whip stitching.

Monk Strap: A wide strap across the instep that buckles on the side of a closed-toed shoe.

Mule: A slip-on shoe with an open back. Mules usually come with low to moderate heels and can be dressy or casual.

Oxfords: A traditional leather dress shoe that laces over the instep. Oxfords are usually black or brown with minimal embellishments (although there may be some brogueing). Oxfords originated in Ireland and Scotland. *See Balmoral.*

Peep Toe: A woman's shoe with a small opening in the toe box that reveals the toes. In all other respects, this is a closed-toe shoe. Peep toe shoes may be dressy or casual; they come with and without heels.

Perforations: *See brogueing.*

Pinking: Zigzag edging used as trim.

Platform Shoe: A shoe with thick soles at the front of the foot. The heel is also high to accommodate the raised forefoot.

Pump: Closed-toed women's dress shoes with a moderate heel. Pumps do not have any straps or fasteners and are normally low-cut.

Saddle Shoes: Shoes made with a swatch of leather sewn in a contrasting color across the instep. The classic saddle shoe, popular during the 1950s, was white at the toe and the back of the shoe and had a black "saddle" that stretched across the instep.

Sandal: A type of footwear characterized by a sole that is held to the foot with strips of leather or other material.

Slide: A shoe with an open toe, open back and band across the forefoot.

Slingbacks: A women's shoe with a strap that encircles the heel. The strap is usually elastic, or it fastens with a buckle to ensure an adjustable fit. Slingbacks may be dressy or casual; they come with and without heels.

Spectators: Shoes that are designed with two contrasting colors. Spectators were popular among jazz musicians in the 1920s. They often sport wingtips or cap toes.

Stiletto: A shoe with a thin heel that is at least 4 inches long.

Wedges: A high-heeled shoe with a heel that extends from the rear of the shoe to the ball of the foot.

Wellington: Pull-on rubber boots designed to keep the feet and lower legs dry.

Wingtip: This shoe type is adorned with a toe cap that is roughly shaped like the letter "W." The toe cap comes to a point at the center (almost like a widow's peak). Wingtip shoes are a popular style for men, although they are sometimes made for women too.

CHAPTER 3

What to Look for in an Athletic Shoe

ATHLETIC SHOES SPORT SOME OF THE FINEST TECHNOLOGY THE SHOEMAKING industry has to offer. Unfortunately, it can be overwhelming to shop for athletic shoes if you are not familiar with the latest terminology and trends. If you find yourself puzzling over the difference between an EVA (ethylene vinyl acetate) and PU (polyurethane) midsole, or wondering exactly what "motion control" means and why it is important, then this is the chapter for you.

In the following pages, you will learn how to:

- find sport specific shoes
- distinguish between running and walking shoes
- purchase athletic shoes that suit your foot type
- identify the five basic types of running shoes

and much more! Whether you are an amateur athlete or burgeoning star, this chapter will guide you in finding athletic shoes that can help you reach your personal best. Ready, set, go!

TIPS FOR PURCHASING ATHLETIC SHOES

✓ **Purchase shoes that cater to your foot type.** Do you have high arches or low arches? Do you over-pronate or supinate? The answers to these questions will determine the type of athletic shoe you should be wearing. Turn to page 4 to learn how to identify your foot type, or flip ahead to page 46 to learn about running shoes designed with specific foot types in mind.

✓ **Purchase running shoes 1/2 size bigger than your normal size.** Athletic shoes run slightly smaller than your average dress or daily-wear shoe. Most people need to increase their shoe size by 1/2 to 2 sizes depending on the type of athletic shoe (running, walking, tennis, etc.) and the shoe brand.

   Also, you want about a thumb's width of space at the front of your shoe in order to accommodate swelling. (Feet tend to swell when you exercise!)

✓ **Buy sport specific shoes.** Different sports place different demands on your body, and sport-specific athletic shoes are designed to meet those different demands. Turn to the next page to read specific footwear guidelines for tennis, basketball, and other sports.

✓ **Use your old athletic shoes as a guide.** By examining the wear on the outsole, you can learn a lot about your stride, foot type, and running style. Over-pronators tend to put more wear on the medial (inside) side of the forefoot of their shoe soles.  Under-pronators tend to put more wear on the lateral (outside) side of the forefoot of their shoe soles. It is best to take your shoes to an expert at your local shoe store for a determination—assuming that you can find an expert at your local shoe store.

✓ **Try on athletic shoes with the proper socks.** Your athletic shoes will fit differently depending on the socks you wear. Be sure to purchase athletic shoes only after trying them on with the proper socks. Look for socks that will absorb moisture. (Not only does this keep feet dry, it can also help prevent blisters!) Acrylic and polyester blends generally work better than cotton.

✓ **Purchase two pairs of shoes at one time.** If you run every day, consider purchasing two pairs of shoes and alternating between them. Purchasing two pairs ensures that your shoes dry thoroughly between runs. It also allows you to stock up on a favorite running shoe before the specific style is replaced. (Note: Most models of running shoes are discontinued every 12 to 15 months, although you can usually find a similar shoe in the same series.)

✓ **Replace running shoes every 300 to 400 miles.** Over time, running shoes lose their ability to cushion and support your feet. Running in flat shoes can lead to complications such as runner's knee and plantar fasciitis.

✓ **Take your time when trying on shoes.** Be prepared to invest time before making a purchase. You can easily spend upward of 45 minutes in an athletic shoe store trying on different styles and brands. If the store has knowledgeable employees, ask someone to help you get a great fit. The best athletic shoe salesmen can determine a lot about the type of shoe you need just by watching you walk and examining your feet.

SPORT-SPECIFIC SHOES

Consider the demands that different physical activities place on your body: Sprinters move forward through space, while tennis players shuffle side-to-side. Basketball players start and stop suddenly in short, explosive movements, while cross-country runners withstand many miles over difficult terrain. It makes sense that different sports would require different shoes!

Of course, it is not necessary to invest in sport-specific shoes for the occasional game of hoops with your buddies. But if you are clocking regular hours each week, then finding a shoe designed specifically for your sport will improve your athletic performance and preserve the health of your feet and body.

Aerobic Shoes

Aerobic shoes should support the body as it makes quick, lateral movements; they should also absorb shock from jumping, running in place and stepping down.

Look for shoes with:

- excellent cushioning beneath the ball of the foot
- rigid heel counters for stability
- lateral support to prevent ankle roll-over
- lightweight soles and uppers

Basketball

Basketball shoes should help the athlete change direction quickly; they should also absorb shock from jumping and protect against ankle injury.

Look for shoes with:

- thick, rigid midsoles for stability
- rigid heel counters for stability
- high tops for ankle protection
- excellent cushioning, particularly in the heel
- deep grooves on the outsole for traction (Note: the "herringbone" tread pattern is ideal)

Cleated Shoes

Cleated shoes are designed for baseball, football and soccer; they should provide the athlete with excellent traction when playing on natural surfaces.

Look for shoes with:

- thin, flexible midsoles
- stability features such as rigid heel counters
- specialty toe boxes to protect the toes and control the ball (soccer)

Note: Athletes can choose between molded (i.e., permanent) and detachable cleats. In general, molded cleats are best for turf and detachable cleats are best for grass.

Cross-Trainers

Cross-trainers are designed to be used with a variety of sports. They incorporate features from running shoes and court shoes.

Look for shoes with:

- more side-to-side mobility than running shoes
- more lateral support than running shoes
- greater flexibility in the forefoot than court shoes

Cycling Shoes

Cycling shoes should help the cyclist maintain good contact with the pedal at all times.

Look for shoes with:

- thin, rigid soles
- good traction
- lightweight soles and uppers
- snug heel cups that hold the heel in place through an entire pedal rotation

Note: Some cycling shoes have cleats that help the foot grip the pedal. Cycling shoes vary depending on whether they are used for road racing, touring, mountain biking, or spinning.

Tennis Shoes

Tennis shoes should support the body as it makes quick, lateral movements; they should also absorb shock and provide excellent traction.

Look for shoes with:

- wide, stable outsoles with a flat bottom for side-to-side mobility
- thin, hard soles for side-to-side mobility
- rigid heel counters for stability
- lateral support to prevent ankle rollover
- padded toe boxes to prevent toe injury
- good ventilation, particularly for play on outdoor courts

Running Shoes

Running shoes should help absorb shock and control pronation. Their design varies widely based on foot type. Please refer to page 46 to learn more about what to look for in running shoes.

Walking Shoes

Walking shoes should help the foot smoothly roll from heel to toe. Some cushioning and motion-control features may be necessary.

Look for shoes with:

- flexible midsoles
- light, flexible cushioning that does not interfere with the foot's stride
- upturned toes and rocker-bottomed soles

WHAT ABOUT PRONATION?

As mentioned in Chapter 1, "How to Get a Good Fit," pronation is your body's way of absorbing shock. The extent to which your body naturally pronates is very important when it comes to choosing a running shoe that will properly support your feet, ankles, knees, and hips.

First a quick refresher: Pronation occurs as your foot strikes the ground and rolls from heel to toe. During this transfer of weight, your arch collapses slightly, and your heel and ankle roll inward. All of these motions together make up **pronation**.

Unfortunately, Mae West was not referring to pronation when she declared: "Too much of a good thing is wonderful!" Too much pronation is bad for the body. The arch flattens almost completely, and the ankle rolls too far inward, putting stress on the bones, ligaments, and muscles of the foot. **Over-pronation** can lead to complications such as plantar fasciitis and runner's knee.

Not enough pronation can also damage the body. People who under-pronate essentially lack cushioning. Their body's limited ability to absorb shock can lead to complications such as shin splints and tendonitis. This phenomenon is referred to as **under-pronation** or **supination**.

The diagram below will help you picture the difference between regular pronation, over-pronation, and supination.

Pronation, Over-Pronation and Supination

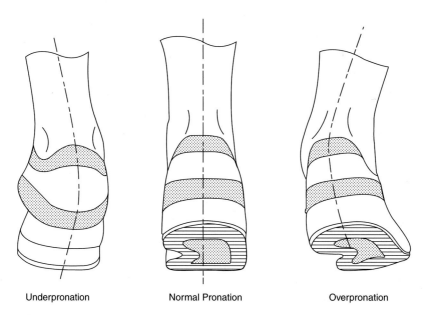

Underpronation   Normal Pronation   Overpronation

A word on Pronation and Arch Height:

Pronation is related to arch height. People with low arches tend to over-pronate, while people with high arches are most often supinators.

Tip

If you need help determining whether you over- or under-pronate, take a close look at an old pair of running shoes. People who wear out the medial side (side toward other foot) of their outsoles first are normally over-pronators; people who wear out the lateral side (side away from other foot) of their outsoles tend to be supinators. But be sure to check with a doctor for a diagnosis or ask an expert shoe salesman to take a look.

THE FIVE BASIC TYPES OF RUNNING SHOES

There are five major types of running shoes. Three of these shoe types—motion control, stability, and cushioned running shoes—are determined by your foot type. If you need help determining your foot type, or refreshing your memory on terms such as pronation, over-pronation, and supination, please refer to Chapter 1 on "How to Get a Good Fit" (pages 2 and 5, respectively). The other two types of running shoes—trail shoes and racing shoes—are determined by the circumstances in which the shoes are to be worn.

Note: Athletic shoes designed for physical activities other than running may also be available with motion control, stability, and cushioning features. For example, it is possible to find a "motion control basketball shoe," or a "stability soccer shoe."

Motion Control

Best for:

- Runners who have low arches or flat feet.
- Runners who are moderate to severe over-pronators.
- Runners who are heavier and need extra support.

Design:

Motion Control shoes are designed to prevent the foot from rolling inward excessively (i.e., over-pronation). They are usually built on a straight last in order to limit over-pronation. Compared to neutral running shoes, motion control shoes will:

- be more rigid
- be heavier
- have a wider outsole
- have a high-density medial post

The **medial post** is a wedge of high-density EVA material[5] that is inserted into the sole of the shoe on the medial side (i.e., the inside of the foot). The dense foam resists compression, and this resistance reduces the amount the foot rolls inward with each stride.

Medial posts come in various sizes and densities depending on the amount of resistance needed. Bigger is not necessarily better: It is possible for a shoe to have a medial post that is too large and too hard for your foot.

Medial posts are easy to spot because they are often made in a contrasting color. They generally run from the heel to the ball of the foot.

Stability

Best for:

- Runners who have medium arches.
- Runners who are mild to moderate pronators.

Design:

Stability shoes offer features found in both motion control and cushioning shoes—but to a lesser extent. The goal is to support the foot without interfering with the foot's natural and healthy pronation tendencies. You can count on stability running shoes for excellent arch

---

5 EVA or ethylene vinyl acetate is a foam commonly used in midsoles of athletic shoes. Please see page 49 of this chapter for more information.

support and midsole cushioning. They correct for slight over-pronation but are not nearly as restrictive as proper motion control shoes. Stability running shoes are usually built on a semi-curved last.

This category of running shoes is best for the majority of runners.

Cushioned

Best for:

- Runners who have high arches.

- Runners who are supinators, or under-pronators.

Design:

Cushioned running shoes are designed to provide the high-arched foot with extra cushioning and excellent shock absorption. These features help compensate for the foot's tendency to under-pronate. Cushioned running shoes are usually built on a curved last in order to encourage pronation. Compared to neutral running shoes, cushioned running shoes will:

- be more flexible.
- have softer midsoles.
- have less medial support.

Trail Shoes

Best for:

- Runners who run off-road.

- Runners who need extra traction.

- Runners who need more durable shoes.

- Runners who need thicker, more durable soles.

Trail shoes are designed for people who need tough shoes that can handle off-road conditions. These shoes will hold up through all kinds of weather and on rough terrains.

You can find trail shoes suited for different foot types.

Racing Shoes

Best for:

- Runners who have no motion control problems.
- Runners who need shoes for fast-paced training or racing.

These shoes have very little to offer in terms of stability, cushioning, or durability features. They are designed to be as lightweight as possible in order to increase the runner's speed. Racing shoes tend to have a low heel and flexible forefoot. They are not recommended for people with injuries or pronation problems.

MIDSOLES: EVA VERSUS PU

When deciding which running shoe to buy, one of the most important features is the midsole. Tucked between the outsole and the insole, the midsole is responsible for absorbing shock each time your foot hits the ground. It can also promote foot stability and correct for conditions such as over-pronation.

Midsoles are generally made from two basic materials: EVA and PU.

EVA, *ethylene vinyl acetate*

This compound is neither plastic nor rubber but foam. Every EVA midsole is made up of thousands of foam bubbles, the same way cells make up a tissue. Each foam bubble is filled with air. The result is a material that is lightweight and flexible.

Every time you land on an EVA midsole, your shoe breathes a little: Air is pushed out of the bubbles as the midsole takes on the body's weight, and then rushes back into the bubbles as your foot leaves the ground.

PU, *polyurethane*

This foam is formally known as polyurethane. It is heavier and denser than EVA, and for these reasons, it is generally less preferred by runners. However, PU midsoles tend to hold up better over time than

EVA midsoles. (The bubbles that make up EVA midsoles eventually lose some of their air permanently.) To summarize: PU midsoles give less bounce in the beginning but their bounce lasts longer.

A Magical Combination

Midsoles are sometimes made with a combination of the two materials. The classic design is to put PU on the outside of the midsole where the shoe receives the most stress and then maintain a light EVA core.

Note: Often shoe companies will use special terms or "company lingo" to describe their midsoles. Notice the "EVA" in Asic's SpEVA® midsole or New Balance's ACTEVA® midsole.

CHAPTER 4

What to Look for in Boots

SOME BOOTS ARE DESIGNED TO PROTECT OUR FEET FROM THE RAIN, from the wear and tear of a 20-mile hike, or from hazards in the workplace. Other boots enable us to glide over snow, fly on a horse's back, or strut down the street in style. And while such boots may not always resemble each other in shape, material, or purpose, they often are designed to take us to the extremities of adventure and fashion.

In this chapter, you will discover how to:

- choose winter boots that are appropriate for your climate
- purchase quality hiking boots
- find work boots suited to your work environment

And much more! Whether you can hardly wait to play in the snow or need a serious pair of boots that will get the job done, this chapter will point you in the right direction.

HIKING BOOT CLASSIFICATION

The first step in purchasing hiking boots is deciding which type of boot best meets your needs. Boots are generally divided into four major categories from Class A to Class D. The best category for any given hiker will depend on that hiker's experience and the types of trips he or she intends to make.

CLASS A | Hiking Shoes or Trail Boots. These boots are best for beginning hikers, or hikers who plan to stick to well-maintained trails. The shoes are made from a combination of leather and a lightweight fabric such as nylon. The shoes are designed to be flexible, and the cut of the shoe is lower than heavy-duty hiking boots.

Trail Running Shoes or Cross Trainers are generally classified as Class A shoes. These heavy-duty running shoes are designed for long-distance runs on well-maintained mountain trails. Hiking Sandals—perfect for low intensity summer excursions—are also Class A shoes.

CLASS B | Cross Hikers or Mid-Weight Boots. These boots are ideal for multi-day hikes on maintained trails or off-trail terrain. The soles of the boots are less flexible than Class A boots, and the boots come up higher around the ankle (for extra support). Class B boots are also made out of slightly stiffer, more durable material than Class A boots, and as a result, they take longer to break in. Nonetheless, mid-weight boots are still manageable for a beginning hiker.

CLASS C | Off-trail Boots or Heavy-Duty Boots. These boots are perfect for off-trail adventures. They are stiffer, higher, and more high-tech than your casual hiking shoe, and they can be too much to handle for an inexperienced hiker. Class C boots generally have a toe cap (for protection), high-tech materials such as Gore-Tex (a waterproof yet breathable material) and additional shock absorption.

CLASS D | Mountaineering Boots. These boots are for the serious mountaineer and are usually used in conjunction with Crampons (steel or aluminum spikes that are used for traction when hiking across snow or ice). They can protect the feet against sub-zero temperatures and may be just what you need if your plan is to scale the Rockies.

CHARACTERISTICS OF QUALITY HIKING BOOTS

Quality hiking boots share many characteristics with quality athletic shoes including excellent arch support and specialty pronation features.

✓ **Thick rubber soles:** The soles of hiking boots are thick, and with good reason! If you felt every rock you stepped on during a 10-mile hike, the soles of your feet would be mighty sore by the day's end.

✓ **Deep tread:** Look for hiking boots with deep tread or lugs. A treaded sole will give you the traction you need when trudging along muddy trails or navigating a steep descent.

✓ **Ankle support:** Uneven trail surfaces make hikers vulnerable to sprained ankles. Look for boots that come up just above the ankle. Boots should also be fairly stiff in this area, providing lateral rigidity that will protect the ankle in case of a fall.

✓ **Lightweight materials:** Hiking experts suggest that every extra pound of boot is equivalent to adding 5 pounds to your pack. High quality boots will be durable *and* lightweight.

✓ **Padded scree collar:** The back of your hiking boots should dip slightly to protect the Achilles tendon from chafing. This collar should be foam padded for comfort.

  Note: It is called a "scree" collar because it is designed to prevent small pebbles and rock fragments, or scree, from slipping inside your boot.

✓ **Hooks above the eyelets:** These metal hooks will help you to cinch laces tightly around the ankle.

✓ **Waterproof or waterproof-able:** As any hiker who has ever been caught in a thunderstorm will tell you, keeping your feet dry is essential to keeping up your spirits and stamina as well as preventing blisters. Look for boots made from waterproof material or from leather or fabric that can easily be waterproofed with the right product. (See page 109 in Chapter 7.)

✓ **Breathable uppers:** No matter how effective hiking boots are at keeping water *out*, they should still be made out of breathable material that allows sweat to evaporate.

✓ **Gusseted tongues:** If you are going to be hiking in wet conditions, look for boots with gusseted tongues. Gusseted tongues are attached to the upper on either side of the tongue with thin flaps known as "gussets." These gussets prevent water or trail debris from entering the boot.

HIKING BOOT SHOPPING TIPS

Like all shoes, it is best to shop for hiking boots in the afternoon when your feet are slightly swollen. Wear the socks you plan on wearing with your boots, and try not to pay too much attention to the boots' numerical size—hiking boots are sized differently than regular shoes.

Loosen the laces and slide your toes to the very front of the boot. You should be able to slide your index finger between your heel and the back of the boot.

Once you have laced up the boots, make sure your toes lie comfortably flat and your heel is not sliding up and down. You should practice walking up and down inclines. In particular, make sure that your toes do not ram into the toe of the boot when going downhill.

If you have the opportunity to visit a hiking equipment store such as REI with knowledgeable staff, it is well worth the extra drive (or hike).

WINTER BOOTS

When winter comes most of us need a little something extra to keep our feet toasty warm as we trudge through the slush. Insulated boots are one of the best ways to beat the winter blues. Please read about the common types of insulation below:

- **Shearling:** Shearling is perhaps most readily recognizable as the material that made UGG® boots so popular. It is made from a tanned sheep's hide that has the wool still attached. The wooly side of the hide is used to line the boots. While shearling boots can be incredibly comfortable, they are best used as casual winter boots that can be worn around town. They are not meant for serious treks in the snow.

- **Polartec®:** Polartec® was originally invented as a lightweight, synthetic version of wool. It is often used to line winter boots and is hydrophobic, that is, it does not retain water.

- **Thinsulate®:** This synthetic fiber is known for keeping feet warm without taking up a lot of space. Not only is Thinsulate® less bulky than natural insulators such as goose down, it also retains its ability to insulate when wet. Most Thinsulate® boots are graded on the amount of Thinsulate® they contain. For example, a boot with 1,000 gram insulation will keep your feet warmer than a boot with 500 gram insulation.

- **Primaloft®:** Used often in Merrell footwear, Primaloft® was originally developed for the U.S. Army after the army requested insulation that remained effective when wet (unlike goose down). Primaloft® is a microfiber, and the most expensive synthetic insulation to manufacture.

In addition to insulation, there are several other features to look for in winter boots. Tall boots with thick rubber soles, good traction and no heel are generally ideal for snowy climates and sub-zero temperatures. But such high-performing boots are not always necessary. Use the flowchart on the next page to determine what type of winter boot is ideal for your climate.

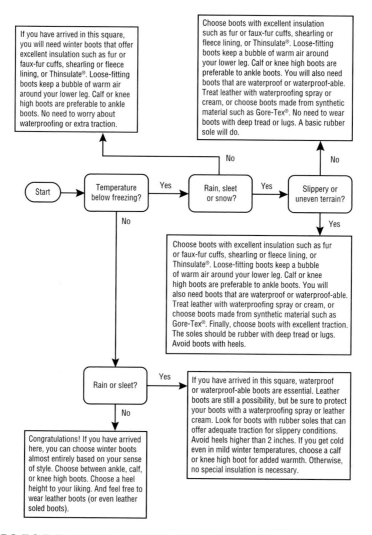

If you have arrived in this square, you will need winter boots that offer excellent insulation such as fur or faux-fur cuffs, shearling or fleece lining, or Thinsulate®. Loose-fitting boots keep a bubble of warm air around your lower leg. Calf or knee high boots are preferable to ankle boots. No need to worry about waterproofing or extra traction.

Choose boots with excellent insulation such as fur or faux-fur cuffs, shearling or fleece lining, or Thinsulate®. Loose-fitting boots keep a bubble of warm air around your lower leg. Calf or knee high boots are preferable to ankle boots. You will also need boots that are waterproof or waterproof-able. Treat leather with waterproofing spray or cream, or choose boots made from synthetic material such as Gore-Tex®. No need to wear boots with deep tread or lugs. A basic rubber sole will do.

Start → Temperature below freezing? —Yes→ Rain, sleet or snow? —Yes→ Slippery or uneven terrain?

No

No   No

Yes

Choose boots with excellent insulation such as fur or faux-fur cuffs, shearling or fleece lining, or Thinsulate®. Loose-fitting boots keep a bubble of warm air around your lower leg. Calf or knee high boots are preferable to ankle boots. You will also need boots that are waterproof or waterproof-able. Treat leather with waterproofing spray or cream, or choose boots made from synthetic material such as Gore-Tex®. Finally, choose boots with excellent traction. The soles should be rubber with deep tread or lugs. Avoid boots with heels.

Rain or sleet? —Yes→ If you have arrived in this square, waterproof or waterproof-able boots are essential. Leather boots are still a possibility, but be sure to protect your boots with a waterproofing spray or leather cream. Look for boots with rubber soles that can offer adequate traction for slippery conditions. Avoid heels higher than 2 inches. If you get cold even in mild winter temperatures, choose a calf or knee high boot for added warmth. Otherwise, no special insulation is necessary.

No

Congratulations! If you have arrived here, you can choose winter boots almost entirely based on your sense of style. Choose between ankle, calf, or knee high boots. Choose a heel height to your liking. And feel free to wear leather boots (or even leather soled boots).

TIPS FOR BUYING BOOTS FOR CHILDREN

When it snows, most children cannot wait to dash outside and explore the winter wonderland. Of course nothing ruins a romp in the snow faster than a pair of wet, freezing feet.

Children in snowy climates will need a good pair of snow boots. Make sure the uppers are waterproof and extend at least to the mid-calf. The boots should also come with a thick, rubber sole that has excellent traction. Additional recommendations include:

✓ **Pull-on boots:** You want your child to be able to put on and take off his or her boots without any assistance. Avoid laces, which can be difficult to manage with cold fingers, and instead opt for something that can be pulled on and off, or with hook-and-loop fasteners such as Velcro®.

✓ **Drawstrings:** Choose boots with a drawstring at the top that can be cinched around your child's leg. This will prevent snow from slipping inside the boot.

✓ **Extra room for snow pants:** Ideally you want to be able to tuck your child's pants or snow pants down into the boot. The goal is to keep the entire lower leg and foot dry.

✓ **Removable liners:** Look for boots with removable liners. This will help you quickly dry the boots after a long day in the snow.

✓ **Extra room for thick socks:** Most children will wear thick socks with their winter boots. You may need to purchase boots that are a half size larger to accommodate the socks.

CHARACTERISTICS OF QUALITY WORK BOOTS

A pair of work boots that will withstand the test of time is an essential tool for workers in many professions. While work boots vary depending on your specific line of work and work environment, there are several basic features that you should look for:

✓ **Reinforced toe box:** Toes are a particularly vulnerable area of your body and a reinforced toe box, or even a steel toe, can help protect you from injury. A boot with a reinforced toe is absolutely essential for professions that involve heavy lifting or power tools.

✓ **Slip resistant soles:** Most quality work boots should have thick, rubber soles with deep tread for excellent traction. If you work in an environment that commonly has wet or oily floors, make sure your boots advertise "slip resistant" soles.

✓ **Molded outsole and upper:** Boots that have the upper and out-sole molded together will last longer than boots that are glued or stitched together.

✓ **Weather appropriate:** If you work outside in cold temperatures, make sure to purchase insulated boots. Choose boots with the appropriate amount of insulation for your climate. (Boots are typically made with anything from 200 to 1,000 grams of insulation material. The amount of insulation in any particular pair of boots should be listed on the boot's label or included somewhere in the packaging materials.) Too much insulation will cause your feet to sweat and can actually make your feet cold. Waterproof boots are necessary for wet climates.

✓ **Breathable materials:** Most quality work boots are made from leather. If you work in a hot climate, you may want to investigate boots with mesh gussets that allow your feet to breathe. In any case, your boots should not be so water-tight that air cannot circulate. This will cause your feet to sweat, which can lead to blisters.

A WORD ON ORTHOPEDIC WORK BOOTS

Work boots are tough, durable boots that can be hard on the feet, especially if you suffer from diabetes or other conditions that can make your feet sensitive to minor injuries. The good news is that orthopedic work boots do exist. In general, they will be able to accommodate orthotics and other orthopedic inserts. They will be made from slightly softer leather that does not require a break in period. And they will have padded tongues and collars for extra comfort and protection.

P. W. Minor makes several different versions of orthopedic work boots. One of these boots, the Hercules, is described as an "Oil Resistant Steel Toe Work Boot," and it offers 25 percent additional depth and

13 percent additional space in the ball of the foot to accommodate orthotics. The boot is made from soft acid-resistant leather.

The shoe company Drew® also makes an orthopedic work boot called the "Big Easy" that may be ideal for someone who wants a light-weight work boot without a steel toe. This boot is extra-wide and has a padded tongue and collar. It is lined with a material specifically de-signed to wick away moisture and keep the feet cool and dry.

These are just two examples of work boots designed for feet that need a little extra comfort and protection. The takeaway message here is that you can still protect your feet in hazardous work environments without punishing them in stiff, unrelenting boots.

CHAPTER 5

What to Look for in an Orthopedic Shoe

FOOT PAIN? KNEE PAIN? BACK PAIN? IT DOES NOT MATTER WHERE IT pinches or aches, orthopedic shoes can relieve pain quickly. But the right pair of shoes offers more than just relief. It can prevent foot deformities and injuries, and in some cases, it can even correct them.

In this chapter, you will discover how to:

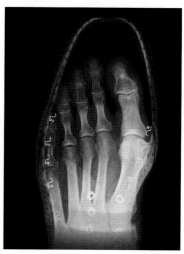

- identify characteristics of quality orthopedic shoes
- distinguish between rigid, soft, and semi-rigid orthotics
- choose orthopedic shoes designed to treat a specific condition

and much more! If you suffer from a common foot deformity or injury, it is time to see how orthopedic shoes can dramatically improve your quality of life.

CHARACTERISTICS OF QUALITY ORTHOPEDIC SHOES

Though orthopedic shoes are often designed to treat specific conditions, there are a few basic characteristics that are consistently important across the board. Look for these key features the next time you go shopping for orthopedic shoes.

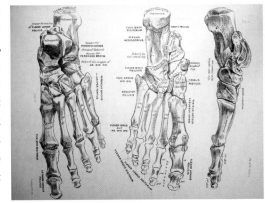

- ✓ **A wide and deep toe box:** Hammertoe, claw toe, corns, calluses, blisters, and bunions are simply a few of the foot deformities that can be caused or aggravated by toe boxes that are too narrow or too shallow. Cramming your toes into a shoe is simply not worth the long-term consequences to your health. Your toes should be able to spread out comfortably in your shoes with wiggle-room to spare. Opt for round or square toes over pointy-toed shoes.

- ✓ **Removable insoles:** Purchasing shoes with removable insoles allows you to change the size of your shoes in order to accommodate the swelling of your feet. It also enables you to replace your shoes' insoles with custom orthotics. Finally, removable insoles work wonders when it comes to drying your shoes quickly and thoroughly. Dry shoes are important when it comes to preventing bacterial or fungal infections such as Athlete's foot or fungal toenail infections.

- ✓ **Firm heel counter:** Heel counters are designed to add stability to the shoe. To check if a shoe has a firm heel counter, press your thumbs against the back of the heel. If the heel bends inward easily, it does not have a firm heel counter. If the heel resists bending, a firm heel counter is present.

- ✓ **Contoured foot bed:** Orthopedic shoes should complement the natural curves of the foot. Contoured foot beds are designed to fit and support your feet in all the crucial places.

✓ **Slight heel:** Heels are sometimes considered a negative feature in shoes for people with foot injuries or deformities, but in some cases, a slight heel is helpful. Look for shoes that provide a subtle lift. Anything from a 1/2 inch to 1 and 1/2 inch heel could be appropriate for your specific condition.

✓ **Rocker bottom sole:** Shoes with a "rocker bottom" sole have an outsole that points slightly upward at the toe and the back of the heel so that the foot rolls smoothly through its stride without putting excessive pressure on the ball of the foot.

Note: Rocker bottom soles are not for everyone. Check with a doctor to make sure that this feature is beneficial for your condition.

✓ **Seamless interior:** Smooth interiors are especially important for people with conditions such as diabetes or lymphedema, or who are vulnerable to minor foot injuries. A seamless interior helps to protect the delicate skin of the foot from friction along the seam line.

✓ **Breathable uppers:** Keeping the foot dry is important when it comes to keeping the foot infection free. Shoes that are made out of breathable materials promote air circulation and keep the shoe free of sweat and other moisture.

✓ **Padded tongue and collar:** An ultra-soft tongue and collar helps to prevent irritation that can lead to minor foot injuries such as blisters and calluses.

ORTHOTICS

Foot or ankle orthotics are devices designed to support, align, or protect the feet and ankles. They also are used to correct or to prevent deformity. Orthotics are sometimes referred to as orthopedic inserts or devices. They can be as simple as a foam insole that you purchase at a drug store or as complex as a brace you have custom-made by a podiatrist.

Orthotics can be classified into three major groups:

Rigid Orthotics

These orthotics are capable of changing the way the foot functions. They are usually made by a podiatrist. The traditional method is to take a plaster cast of the patient's foot, but many podiatrists use high-tech methods such as laser systems or semi-weight bearing foam.[6] The goal of all these methods is to provide the patient with a custom-fit. Most rigid orthotics are made from a hard plastic or compressed fiber.

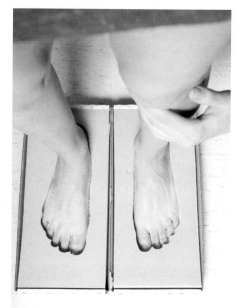

Rigid orthotics can be used to prevent extreme over-pronation, make uneven limbs level when wearing shoes, and address pain in the lower back and upper legs.

A person has casts made of their feet while standing on semi-weight bearing foam.

Soft Orthotics

These orthotics are designed to absorb shock and alleviate pressure in key points of the foot and ankle. They are made from soft, pliable materials such as cork, leather, foam, and rubber. Some insoles are even made from viscoelastic polymers, a gel-like substance.

Soft orthotics can be used to treat plantar fasciitis, runner's knee, cavus foot (high arch), and foot problems related to diabetes.

---

6 Another method involves the patient standing on a bed with small rods that correspond to the sole of the foot. The way the rods move when the patient stands on them provides the podiatrist with information about the foot's shape.

Semi-Rigid Orthotics

These orthotics are designed to enhance balance and agility in the foot and ankle. They are primarily used by athletes, or people who exert an above-average amount of stress on the bones of their feet. Semi-rigid orthotics are made from alternating layers of soft and rigid material.

Semi-rigid orthotics are usually sport-specific. They are also sometimes used by people whose careers force them to be on their feet all day.

No matter which type of orthotic you use, it is important to adjust your shoes to accommodate the orthotic. Sometimes people go up an entire size. Remember: When shopping for new shoes, bring your orthotics with you.

Also, it is important to note that orthotics can do as much harm as good. If you overcorrect for a certain condition, you could end up exacerbating the condition or creating a new problem. Most of the orthopedic insoles that are available over-the-counter are safe to use without consulting a podiatrist first. But if you notice any foot, ankle, knee, leg, or back pain, it is best to check in with your doctor. Orthotics that significantly change the way the foot functions are only available through a podiatrist—and with good reason!

ORTHOPEDIC SHOES BY CONDITION

As mentioned earlier, what you need out of your orthopedic shoe will depend on the specific needs of your feet. Different foot types, conditions, injuries, and deformities all require slightly different combinations of key orthopedic features.

Use the catalogue below as a basic guide when shopping for shoes suitable for a particular condition.

Achilles Tendinitis

Achilles tendinitis occurs when the Achilles tendon becomes inflamed or irritated. It is often related to sports injuries, particularly overtraining, or a sudden increase in physical exercise. A sore and swollen Achilles tendon can also be a sign that shoes are not supporting the feet properly.

Avoid shoes with:

- little to no cushioning in the heel
- heels higher than 1 and 1/2 inches
- no heel
- little to no arch support

Look for shoes with:

- lots of cushioning, particularly in the heel
- a heel somewhere between 1/2 inch and 1 and 1/2 inches
- excellent arch support
- motion control features (see page 46 for more details)

Notes: Heel lifts are available at your local drugstore and your podiatrist's office. By adjusting the size of your heel, you can change the amount your Achilles tendon stretches. A higher heel means a shorter tendon. This can help you recover from injury, but it also can permanently shorten your tendon. A lower heel means a more stretched tendon. Ask your doctor for details.

Arthritis

Arthritis is characterized by swelling and inflammation in the joints. There are several types of arthritis. The condition can be genetic, the result of disease or infection, or it can develop over time due to injury or general wear and tear. Although arthritis can strike at any age, it is the leading cause of disability among people who are over 55.

Avoid shoes with:

- little to no cushioning
- little to no shock absorption
- shallow or narrow toe boxes

Look for shoes with:

- lots of cushioning
- excellent shock absorption

- excellent arch support
- wide and deep toe boxes
- rocker bottom soles
- removable insoles for easy size adjustment
- hook and loop fasteners (e.g., Velcro®) for easy size adjustment

Notes: Arthritis is often accompanied by corollary deformities such as bunions, hammertoe, etc. Choose shoes that will prevent these deformities from forming, or accommodate them if they have already developed.

Bunions

A bunion is a common foot deformity characterized by a pronounced bump that develops at the base of the big toe. The bump is actually the enlargement of the joint near the first metatarsal bone. Bunions are sometimes accompanied by a condition known as *hallux valgus*, which occurs when the big toe angles toward the little toe instead of pointing straight ahead. Bunions are a hereditary condition that can be exacerbated by wearing ill-fitting footwear.

Avoid shoes with:

- pointed toes
- narrow or shallow toe boxes
- heels higher than 1 inch

Look for shoes with:

- square or round toes
- deep and wide toe boxes
- seamless interiors to prevent irritation
- slight heels

Notes: Sometimes people with bunions choose to go up a shoe size in order to accommodate the deformity.

There are a variety of orthotic devices for people with bunions including toe separators, bunion cushions, and bunion splints.

Cavus Foot
Please see "High Arches."

Claw Toe
Please see "Hammertoe."

Club Foot
Clubfoot, or Giles Smith Syndrome, is a birth defect that causes one or both feet to turn inward so that the toes point to the middle of the body. The feet also appear as if they are rolling over, so that the tops of the feet are where the soles of the feet should be. Children affected by clubfoot tend to have feet that are shorter and broader than the average child's feet. Muscles in the calf may also be affected, resulting in the lower leg being disproportionately small.

Special shoes exist for people with club feet but recommendations are best left to a doctor. Often children who are undergoing the Ponsetti method of treatment will use a combination of casts, splints, and orthopedic shoes.

Children who are successfully treated for club foot are more likely to end up with feet of two different sizes. The former club foot tends to be significantly smaller than the normal foot. Please see page 16 in Chapter 1 for more information on mismatched feet.

Diabetic Foot
The combination of poor circulation and decreased sensation caused by neuropathy makes it difficult for people with diabetic foot to detect foot pain. Small cuts, blisters, and other foot injuries often go unnoticed and therefore untreated. Infections develop more easily and are harder to treat without the proper circulatory defense. Diabetic foot can lead to foot deformities such as calluses, corns, bunions, and hammertoe. In more serious cases, foot ulcers can develop on the foot, and

under extreme circumstances, amputation may be necessary in order to prevent an infection from spreading to the rest of the body.

Avoid shoes with:

- narrow or shallow toe boxes
- little to no cushioning
- heels higher than 1 inch

Look for shoes with:

- wide and deep toe boxes
- removable insoles for a flexible fit
- rocker soles
- firm heel counters for increased stability
- hook and loop (e.g., Velcro®) fasteners for easy size adjustments
- seamless interiors

Notes: People with diabetes often benefit from orthotics designed to protect and support the foot. Inserts made with a material called Plastazote® change shape based on heat and pressure. This enables the insert to accommodate specific hot spots and pressure points.

Flat Feet or Fallen Arches

Flat feet (also known as fallen arches) is a common condition that occurs when the foot's arch collapses. Some people are born with flat feet, while others develop it as they age. People with low or fallen arches are generally over-pronators. (For more information on pronation, please refer to page 5.)

Avoid shoes with:

- little to no arch support
- excessive cushioning
- a soft, flexible fit

Look for shoes with:

- good arch support
- motion–control or stability features (please see page 46 for more information)
- a firm heel counter for added stability
- a sizable medial post
- a straight last

Notes: Over-the-counter and prescription orthotics are readily available for people with flat feet or low arches.

Hammertoe

Hammertoe is a common foot deformity that occurs when the middle joint of the toe becomes bent. If the upper joint is bent, the condition is technically referred to as mallet toe. If both joints are bent, the condition is classified as claw toe. Hammertoe is caused by muscle/tendon imbalance in the lesser toes; it is sometimes linked to wearing ill-fitting footwear.

Avoid shoes with:

- narrow or pointed toes
- shallow toe boxes
- heels higher than 1/2 inch

Look for shoes with:

- deep, wide and square toe boxes
- slight heels (approximately 1/2 inch)

Notes: Open-toed shoes sometimes help to relieve pressure on the deformity.

Heel Pain
Please see "Plantar Fasciitis."

High Arches

A foot with a high arch has an arch or instep that is extremely pronounced. Most of the body's weight rests on the ball of the foot and the heel, with the arch off the floor. This condition is less common than flat feet or normal arches, and it is sometimes linked to underlying orthopedic or neurological conditions.

Avoid shoes with:

- little to no shock absorption
- little to no cushioning
- little to no arch support
- extensive stability features such as a medial post, heel counter, etc.

Look for shoes with:

- excellent shock absorption
- lots of cushioning
- good arch support
- soft midsoles
- a "flexible fit"

Notes: Orthotics are widely used to cope with high arches. Sometimes ankle braces are also needed; alternatively, wearing a high-top shoe can give the ankle extra support.

High arches are sometimes accompanied by corollary deformities such as calluses, corns, and hammertoe. Choose shoes that will prevent these deformities from forming or accommodate them if they have already developed.

Lymphedema

Lymphedema is a condition that causes swelling in the arms and legs. It occurs when the body retains interstitial fluid[7] (usually due to a blockage in the lymphatic system) instead of draining the fluid properly. In rare

---

7 Interstitial fluid is the fluid that bathes and surrounds cells in the body.

cases, people are born with lymphedema. More commonly, people acquire it after surgery, trauma, or radiation treatments for various cancers.

Avoid shoes with:

- little to no cushioning
- little to no arch support
- narrow or shallow toe boxes
- open toes or exposed heels
- heels higher than 1/2 inch

Look for shoes with:

- wide and deep toe boxes
- mesh above the toes for breathability
- removable insoles for adjustable size
- hook and loop fastenings for adjustable size

Notes: Shoes that expose the foot should be avoided at all costs. That means no flip-flops, sandals, slip-ons, or backless shoes. Shoes for people with lymphedema should not be tight; it is important to accommodate the foot at its largest size.

Mallet Toes
Please see "Hammertoe."

Metatarsalgia
Metatarsalgia is a painful condition that is localized in the metatarsal region of the foot (i.e., the ball of the foot). It occurs when the metatarsal heads become inflamed, and it is often caused by repeated stress on the ball of the foot.

Avoid shoes with:

- narrow or shallow toe boxes
- pointed toes

- little to no cushioning
- little to no arch support
- heels higher than 1/2 inch

Look for shoes with:

- extra cushioning, particularly beneath the ball of the foot
- excellent arch support
- rocker bottom soles

Notes: People with metatarsalgia often benefit from purchasing shock-absorption gel inserts. The more general goal is to remove excess pressure from the ball of the foot. This means no high heels, lots of cushioning, and shoes that allow the foot to smoothly roll from heel to toe without putting pressure on the metatarsal area (e.g., shoes with rocker bottom soles).

Plantar Fasciitis

Plantar fasciitis is a condition that causes extreme arch and heel pain. It occurs when the plantar fascia, the thick fibrous tissue that stretches from your heel along the bottom of your foot to your toes, is stretched beyond its limits.

Avoid shoes with:

- no arch support
- little to no cushioning
- a heel higher than 1 and 1/2 inches
- no heel

Look for shoes with:

- a slight heel (1/2 to 1 and 1/2 inch)
- excellent arch support
- excellent cushioning
- rocker bottom soles

Notes: Doctors can help you find orthotics that will more evenly distribute your weight across the bottoms of your feet.

Polio

Polio is a viral infectious disease. It attacks the nervous system, which in turn, can lead to certain muscle groups becoming paralyzed. Foot deformities and conditions commonly associated with polio include flat feet, high arches, hammertoe, bunions, and claw toe. Please refer to these specific conditions for more information.

Psoriasis

Psoriasis is a chronic autoimmune disease that affects the skin, nails, and joints. It causes scales to form on the skin (known as psoriatic plaques) and can cause pain in the joints. Psoriasis is most common on the elbows and knees, but it also can affect the hands and feet. In addition to psoriatic plaques, psoriasis on the feet can include blisters, cracking, and swelling.

Avoid shoes with:

- synthetic materials such as plastic that cause the feet to sweat
- narrow or shallow toe boxes
- pointed-toes

Look for shoes with:

- breathable uppers that promote air circulation
- wide and deep toe boxes
- removable insoles for a flexible fit

Notes: It is also a good idea to avoid nylons or socks made of synthetic materials. The goal is to keep feet cool and dry.

Trauma

This heading covers any kind of trauma to the foot, toes, or ankles. It includes breaks, bruises, or sprains; it also includes foot, toe, or ankle surgery.

Avoid shoes with:

- little to no cushioning
- little to no shock absorption
- narrow or shallow toe boxes
- pointed-toes
- open toes or exposed heels

Look for shoes with:

- excellent cushioning
- removable insoles for size adjustment
- hook-and-loop (e.g., Velcro®) fasteners for size adjustment
- covered toes and heels for protection

Notes: If your foot undergoes any kind of trauma, it may be a good idea to go barefoot while the foot recovers. You want to avoid forcing your foot into a shoe too soon. Once you are ready to be on your feet again, look for shoes that provide excellent cushioning and can accommodate swelling. Athletic and orthopedic shoes tend to provide a good combination of support and protection.

CHAPTER 6

How to Spot Counterfeits

WITH THE EXPLOSION OF ONLINE MARKETPLACES, COUNTERFEIT SHOES have become more unavoidable than ever! It takes shopping smarts to get a great deal on a pair of designer shoes *and* avoid sellers trying to cheat you out of an authentic product.

In this chapter, you will discover how to:

- spot warning signs in sellers' online profiles

- protect yourself from counterfeit scams

- look for hallmarks of authenticity in various designer products

And much more! It is possible to find great deals and great designer shoes online, as long as you shop with caution.

RULES TO SHOP BY

*How to Find Authentic Designer
Shoes Online*

$$$ Price

Like it or not, designer shoes are expensive. Sorry to dash your hopes, but if a shoe that usually costs 400 dollars is offered for a mere 89.99, the deal is probably too good to be true. The same goes for those "70% off!" sales. React to low prices with skepticism.

It is possible to find relatively affordable second-hand designer shoes, but you should vet these vendors just as thoroughly as you would a discount Internet site. Ask the second-hand vendor for the original paper tags and shoe box. If they no longer have these items, carefully check the shoes' labels.

Workmanship

Designer shoes are expensive for a reason! The quality of the shoes should be top notch, and a respectable vendor will take complaints regarding the shoes' quality very seriously. Be suspicious of traces of glue. (Authentic designer shoes are generally stitched together.) Inspect the shoe's stitching, its heel, and its insole. Pay close attention to the shoe's label. The label should be well-aligned and precisely stitched to the shoe.

Inconsistent Merchandise

Most Web sites or vendors that sell authentic designer shoes will focus on this niche market. It is a bad sign when you see a Web site offering shoes as well as perfume and kitchen appliances. Or if you see a seller whose merchandise ranges from $5.99 Kmart brand jellies to $500 Gucci pumps.

Feedback

Carefully examine a seller's feedback. If there are complaints regarding service or quality of product, stay away. Occasionally vendors of counterfeit goods will be exposed by an unhappy customer. But be careful! The best counterfeit sellers have excellent feedback, because they are able to successfully fool their customers even after the fake shoes have arrived.

Here is another common trick: Some vendors of counterfeit goods build up positive feedback ratings by selling a lot of little items before launching their big scams.

In conclusion, a seller's feedback rating is a great place to start, but it will not definitively indicate whether or not you can trust the seller.

 Shipping Costs

Most counterfeit shoes are manufactured in Asia, so it is no surprise that many counterfeit vendors have to ship their merchandise from this part of the world. However, these vendors often try to disguise this fact. If a vendor claims to be based in Europe or the United States but attempts to charge you 50 dollars for shipping, it may be a red flag that the shoes are actually coming from somewhere farther afield.

 No Returns

Do not purchase shoes online or through a secondhand market that has a "No Returns" policy. You should be able to return the shoes if you inspect them at home and are not satisfied with the product.

Common (and Fake!) Excuses Vendors Use to Explain Why Designer Shoes Have No Labels

Authentic designer shoes should come with labels and paper tags. Here are some common, and most likely fake excuses that vendors of counterfeit shoes may use to convince potential buyers that the shoes are real despite the absence of tags or labels.

Vendor: The shoes don't have labels or tags because they come directly from the manufacturer.

➡ *Think Fast:* Designer shoes are not sold directly from the manufacturer, especially not at discount prices or in small quantities. (Different rules may apply if you were, for example, purchasing 100 pairs of Gucci pumps.)

Vendor: We remove the labels before shipping.

➡ *Think Fast:* Why would a vendor of designer shoes *ever* do this? These shoes are valuable because people want to show off that coveted designer label. Cutting off the label on a Gucci pump is like blotting out Da Vinci's signature on the Mona Lisa. There is no innocent explanation.

Vendor: We remove the labels on secondhand merchandise.

➡ *Think Fast:* It is true that labels are often altered when designer shoes are sold secondhand, but they should not be removed. The standard practice is either to cut the label, or draw a black line through it.

Vendor: The shoes do not come with labels or tags because they are a sample pair.

➡ *Think Fast:* This excuse covers the vendor's tail on two ends. First, he explains that there are no tags because the shoe is a sample, and second, he creates a way to account for any minor differences you might notice between the "sample" shoe and the designer item sold through the regular marketplace. If a vendor were able to get his hands on a sample designer shoe, there would be some kind of "sample" label.

A Closer Look: Designer Shoes Made in China

The fact that "American" or "European" shoes are made in China is no secret. One of the most effective ways to cut costs is to move the base of operation overseas, and China provides an appealing environment in which to set up shop. One in three Nike sneakers comes with a "Made in China" sticker. But this kind of candidness is more complicated for designer brands such as Chanel, Prada, and Armani that have built their companies on the cornerstone of European craftsmanship. Customers spend extra money on a designer shoe because they want a product crafted by an artisan who knows and loves the art of shoemaking, not by a factory worker in China.

An increasing number of designer shoes are manufactured in China. But this does not mean you will find a tag inside your shoe saying so.

So how do these name brands get away with labeling their shoes as "Made in Italy" when they are actually "Made in China"? The brands benefit from very flexible labeling laws that base a product's label on the final point of production. For example, a shoe may be mostly manufactured in China but have its leather sole attached in Italy. And voila! The shoe is legally "Made in Italy".

That is not to say that designer shoes now manufactured in China are of a lesser quality than designer shoes previously manufactured in Europe. The claim is that shoemakers in China are fast *and* precise. They still produce quality shoes—just in less time and for less money.

A Consequence of Outsourcing: The Counterfeit Market

Stopping the sale and production of counterfeit shoes is more complicated than ever. This is partly because it is becoming more difficult for a consumer to tell a fake from an authentic shoe. And with good reason!

Most European and American shoe companies manufacture their products overseas. By outsourcing the production of their footwear to factories in Asia, these companies give up some control over the design-knowledge that makes an Armani or Prada or even Nike shoe special in the first place. The result is the emergence of the "third shift," also known as the "ghost shift" or "midnight shift." Factories that are licensed by a company to produce brand-name sneakers make shoes for

that company during the day; then at night, these same factories produce an extra thousand pairs of shoes to be sold on the black market
as counterfeits. These "third shift" shoes may be made out of cheaper
materials, but they are made on the same equipment and sometimes by
the same people. As a result, the counterfeits are extremely difficult to
distinguish from an authorized version of the shoe.

This kind of problem is one of the risks that major shoe companies
take when they decide to manufacture their products overseas. However, the companies are saving enough money by outsourcing that it is
well worth the risk.

Verification of Authenticity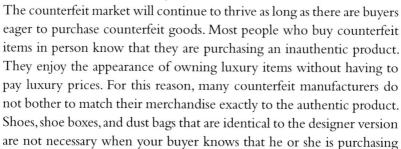

The counterfeit market will continue to thrive as long as there are buyers
eager to purchase counterfeit goods. Most people who buy counterfeit
items in person know that they are purchasing an inauthentic product.
They enjoy the appearance of owning luxury items without having to
pay luxury prices. For this reason, many counterfeit manufacturers do
not bother to match their merchandise exactly to the authentic product.
Shoes, shoe boxes, and dust bags that are identical to the designer version
are not necessary when your buyer knows that he or she is purchasing
a fake.

The retail of counterfeit shoes online has brought a whole other
dimension to the counterfeit marketplace. Suddenly vendors are able
to dupe unsuspecting buyers who think they are getting an incredible
online deal. Photos of authentic designer items are used to advertise
fakes, and often the buyer does not realize the mistake until the shoes
have arrived in the mail.

Shopping Online
Shopping for designer items online requires shopping smarts. The following pages provide you with checklists and general guidelines for
some of the most commonly counterfeited brands and shoes including
Chanel Cambon ballerina flats, Nike Air Jordans, and UGG® boots.

These checklists are designed to help get you started. Do not be
afraid to ask online vendors additional detailed questions about their
products. It is perfectly acceptable to ask sellers on eBay and other
online marketplaces to send detailed pictures of the shoe's label, sole,

and other crucial areas. Honest vendors should be happy to verify the authenticity of their merchandise.

Important Notice Regarding the Following Information

Most vendors of designer merchandise refuse to answer questions regarding authenticity because they do no want to provide counterfeiters with information that potentially could help them produce even more convincing counterfeit products. Consequently, it is difficult to obtain definitive information regarding current logos, labels, and packaging information.

In addition, designer logos, labels, and packaging are constantly changing and are not necessarily consistent from season to season or between different styles of footwear.

As a result, we would like to stress that the following pages are not meant to be the final word on what passes as authentic and what does not. The designer companies themselves are the only definitive authority on their merchandise and trademarks. Instead, use this guide as a handy helper. The photographs are examples only. Your authentic product may not match them exactly. The checklists and guidelines are based on authentic products that we have inspected, but they do not account for every authentic designer product out there.

Chanel

Cambon Ballerina Flats

Counterfeit versions of Chanel's Cambon ballerina flats have flooded the online market. Extra caution is required when shopping online for this particular style of Chanel shoe.

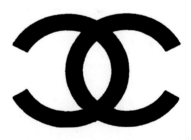

Inside the Shoe:

❑ Does the label inside the shoe read "CHANEL"? Note: If you see a Cambon ballerina flat labeled "CC," it is a fake. Also, there should be no extraneous lettering on the labels such as "Made in Italy" or "Made in France."

❑ If the flats are white, pink, or tan, is the label black?

❑ If the flats are black, is the label white?

The Sole of the Shoe:

❏ Is the heel made of plastic?

❏ Is the heel stamped with "CHANEL" and "Made in Italy?" Note: If the heel is stamped with "CC," the shoe is a fake.

❏ Is the word "CHANEL" printed in big, bold lettering underneath the plastic? Note: This lettering must be printed *underneath* the plastic. It should not be part of the plastic or printed on top of the plastic.

❏ Is the word "CHANEL" written in big, bold lettering?

❏ If the flats are black or white, is the "CHANEL" label hot pink?

❏ If the flats are tan or pink, is the "CHANEL" label black?

❏ If the flats are special edition flats (i.e., white with the python design or silver), is the "CHANEL" label orange?

The Packaging of the Shoe:

❏ Is the shoe box black?

❏ Is the word "CHANEL" written in capital letters across the top of the box? Is the lettering parallel to the box's longer side?

❏ Is the dust bag black with white "CHANEL" lettering?

Note: Genuine Chanel Cambon Ballerina Flats do not come with a statement of authenticity. Yours shouldn't either!

Here is an example of an authentic Chanel shoe box and dust bag. Note how the brand name "CHANEL" is written in capital letters parallel to the long side of the box. Pay attention to the particular font used by the Chanel brand, and how the lettering on the box matches the lettering on the dust bag.

This Chanel high heel is in no way a doppelganger for the Chanel Cambon Ballerina flats. (You will note the presence of the "CC" logo and the description "Made in Italy"—both details conspicuously absent on the flats.) However, you can still glean a sense of what an authentic Chanel logo looks like when printed on the insole of a shoe.

Christian Dior

If you are shopping for Christian Dior shoes, you are likely to find a label on the shoe's insole that depicts an ornate shield shape surrounding the words "Christian Dior." The words "Christian Dior" are perpendicular to the length of the shoe, with the word "Christian" toward the heel above the word "Dior" toward the toe.

This label differs from an alternate, and most likely older, Dior logo, which you can see in the photograph above. This logo depicts a large "Dior" with an uppercase "D" and lowercase "ior." Notice how "Dior is written along the length of the shoe, with the D at the heel and "r" toward the toe.

The Sole of the Shoe:

Shoes with the "Dior" label, as opposed to the ornate shield design, should have the same "Dior" stamped onto the sole of the shoe. The words "MADE IN ITALY" should also be stamped on the sole.

The Shoe's Packaging:

The photograph above is an example of an authentic Dior shoe box and dust bag. This particular box depicts the "Dior" label, as opposed to the ornate shield design. Note that the word "Dior" on the box runs parallel to the shorter side of the box.

Note: Dior shoes do not come with authenticity cards!

Christian Louboutin

Inside the Shoe:

❑ Does the "Christian Louboutin" trademark have "hristian" in block letters, "Louboutin" in cursive script, and the "L" in "Louboutin also serving as the "C" in "Christian"

❑ Is the "Christian Louboutin" trademark located in the heel area of the insole?

❑ Is the word "Louboutin" significantly largely than the word "Christian"?

❑ Is "Paris" printed on the insole? It should be printed in the midfoot area (near the arch) and centered.

The Sole of the Shoe:

❑ Is the sole of the shoe the distinctive Louboutin red?

❑ Is the "Christian Louboutin" trademark described above stamped onto the sole? (Note: The brand name should be identical to the brand printed on the insole.)

❑ Are the words "MADE IN ITALY" printed above the shoe's size?

❑ If you hold the shoe toe up, is the brand name upside down?

The Shoe's Packaging:

❑ Is the dust bag the same red as the shoes' soles?

❑ Does the brand name on the dust bag match the brand name on the shoe box?

Dolce & Gabbana

Inside the Shoe:

❑ Is the brand name "DOLCE & GABBANA®" printed on the insole of the shoe? (Note: The brand name should be written in capital letters and an ampersand should always be used—never the word "and.")

❑ Is the brand name written along the length of the shoe? The "D" should be at the heel and the final "A" should be toward the toe.

❑ Is the ampersand (&) smaller than the letters in the words "DOLCE" and "GABBANA®"?

❑ Is "MADE IN ITALY" printed underneath the brand name?

❑ Is there a registered trademark (®) just above the last "A" in "GABBANA®"?

The Sole of the Shoe:

Depending on the style of shoe, the "DOLCE & GABBANA®" brand name can either be engraved onto the bottom of the sole or engraved onto a metal plate, which is screwed to the bottom of the sole. In either case, be sure to check the lettering's font, size, and spelling.

Notice how even when the brand name is engraved on the metal plate, it retains its salient characteristics: capital letters, small ampersand, and a distinctive font.

Gucci

Inside the Shoe:

❑ Does your Gucci shoe have an eight-digit serial number? This number should be printed inside the shoe on the shoe's lining next to the shoe size.

❑ Does your Gucci shoe have the word "GUCCI" stamped inside the shoe near the heel?

❑ Is there a smaller stamp that says "made in Italy" printed below the brand name?

The Sole of the Shoe:

❑ Does your Gucci shoe have the words "GUCCI" and "made in Italy" stamped on the sole of the shoe? (Note: Sometimes men's shoes have the brand name engraved on a silver plate.)

❑ Is the sole well made? Is it made from the correct materials? (**Tip:** Look up your shoe on the official Gucci Web site to identify the correct material of the sole. Most Gucci dress shoes will be made with leather soles. Athletic shoes as well as some flats and heels are made with rubber soles.)

The Shoe's Packaging:

This picture is an example of an authentic Gucci shoe box and dust bag. Boxes and bags can come in a variety of colors. The Gucci lettering is often metallic. Do not worry if your box and bag differ from the picture at the right. What is most important is that the lettering on the box and bag match the distinctive Gucci logo.

Jimmy Choo

Inside the Shoe:

❑ Is there a neat row of stitching on the top and bottom sides of the label? (Note: If the label is simply inserted into a slit in the insole with no stitching, the shoe is most likely a fake.)

○ Does the label say "JIMMY CHOO"?

○ Is the lettering uppercase?

○ Is the font correct?

○ Is the "OO" in Choo upright? (Note: If the "OO" is italicized, the shoe is most likely a fake.)

○ Is the city name "LONDON" printed in a smaller size below the brand name?

The Sole of the Shoe:

❑ Is the brand name "JIMMY CHOO" stamped on the sole?

❑ Is the city name "London" stamped in smaller lettering beneath the brand name?

❑ Is "MADE IN ITALY" stamped right above the shoe's size?

❑ Some Jimmy Choo shoes with leather soles have the words "VERO CUOIO" (Italian for "real leather") stamped on the soles of the shoe. If this is true of your shoes, are the words "VERO CUOIO" located inside a shield? Do they take up almost all of the space inside the shield?

The Shoe's Packaging:

This photo is an example of an authentic Jimmy Choo shoe box and dust bag. Notice how the color of the shoe box and dust bag match, and how the text is oriented the same way on both box and bag (i.e., parallel to the longer side). Do not be alarmed if your box  and bag differ from this photo. What is most important is the integrity and consistency of the "JIMMY CHOO" logo.

Refer to the authentic Jimmy Choo shoe below. You can even read the care card that comes with new Jimmy Choo shoes.

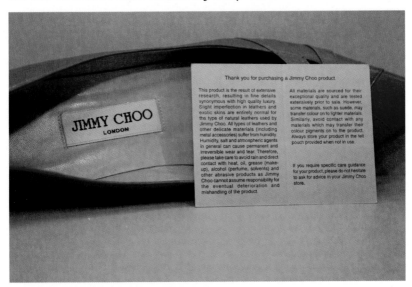

A final word on Jimmy Choo Couture:
Changing Times in the Designer World

Believe it or not, Jimmy Choo shoes are no longer designed by Jimmy Choo! The designer sold his share of the company in 2001. If you want a pair of shoes designed by Jimmy Choo himself, you will have to visit Paddington in London, England and shop for Jimmy Choo Couture.

Manolo Blahnik
Inside the Shoe:

- ❏ Does your Manolo Blahnik have a label stitched to the insole?
- ❏ Is the label well-aligned?
- ❏ Is it stitched on all four sides?
- ❏ Is the brand name spelled correctly? Is it printed in capital letters? (Note: Shoes from the "My Favorites" collection may sport a label with Mr. Blahnik's signature.)

The Sole of the Shoe:

- ❏ Is the sole of the shoe leather?

The Shoe's Packaging:

- ❏ Is the shoe box white with black lettering?
- ❏ Is "MANOLO BLAH-NIK" spelled correctly? Is it in the correct font?
- ❏ Is the dust bag white with black lettering?

Tip
Unlike other shoe brands, Manolo Blahnik shoes do not have embossed serial numbers. If you see an embossed serial number on any part of the shoe, then the shoe is probably a fake.

Nike Air Jordans

Owning a pair of Air Jordans has long been a symbol of social status. The shoes are expensive, which means that people will go to great lengths to own a pair. It also means that there is an army of counterfeit sellers who specialize in Air Jordans.

The Jumpman Logo:

- ❏ Is the basketball on the right side of the logo (i.e., your right)?
- ❏ Is the jumping Jordan placed between the "R" and "D" of the word "Jordan"?
- ❏ Does the arm with the ball veer to the right of the logo?

The Shoe's Packaging:

- ❏ Does the production number of the shoes' tag match the production number printed on the box?
- ❏ Are the shoes wrapped in brown paper? (*Not* tissue paper.)

Note: The best advice for spotting a counterfeit Air Jordan is to do your research ahead of time. Nike has released many versions of this shoe and each version is unique. Find a photo of the shoes online at Nike's Web site and compare your shoes to it. Color, material, details like stripes or the placement of the Nike "swoosh" should all be examined carefully. A key feature to examine is the color of the shoe's sole. Several manufacturers of fake Air Jordans neglect this area of the shoe.

Prada
Inside the Shoe:

- ❑ Does the label or stamp read "PRADA" with "Made in Italy" printed in smaller text?
- ❑ Is the word "PRADA" in all caps? Is it written in the correct font?
- ❑ If the shoe is a sports shoe, does it have a removable insole?
  - ○ Is there an additional "PRADA" logo beneath the removable insole?
  - ○ Is the second logo located in the heel area?

This photograph is an example of the logo on an authentic Prada women's dress shoe.

The Shoe's Packaging:
Please note that the following information is only applicable to Prada sports shoes.

- ❑ Is the logo located on the side of the box (i.e., not the top)?
- ❑ Is the brand name accompanied by information about the size, price, and model of the shoes?
- ❑ Do the shoes come with a silver sleeper bag?
- ❑ Is the logo on the bag red? Is the drawstring of the bag silver?

Here is an example of a genuine Prada shoe box and dust bag for a woman's dress shoe. Do not be alarmed if your box and bag differ from the one pictured.

Additional Features:
Prada sports shoes often have an embossed upside-down triangle (the traditional Prada logo). This triangle is often attached to the shoe's tongue or the back of the heel.

If your Prada shoes come with the triangle logo, verify that it has the following features:

❑ Does the logo read "Prada" on the top line?

❑ Are the words "MILANO" and "DAL 1913" printed below the brand name? **Tip:** Double-check the spelling of these words as well as the date. (It is 1913 *not* 1931!)

❑ Is the date written on what looks like a scroll or ribbon?

❑ Is a coat of arms depicted below the date?

Timberland

Inside the Shoe:

❑ Is there a style number inside the shoe? It should either be listed under the tongue or along the inside of the upper. It is usually listed next to the shoe's size.

❑ Is the style number five digits long?

❑ **Note:** The number 10061 is the style number of the classic yellow Timberland boot. If you see this style number on any shoe other than the classic Timberland, you are probably looking at a fake.

❑ Is the shoe size listed inside the shoe an American size? All Timberlands come in American sizes. They can either be listed as "W" for wide or "M" for medium.

The Shoe's Tags:

❑ Is there a paper tag attached to the shoe's eyelets?

Note: The tag should not have a barcode on it. It should also not say "Genuine Timberland" or be made out of cardboard.

The Shoe's Packaging:

❑ Is the style number listed on the shoe box? Does it match the style number listed inside the shoe?

Note: Always be sure to check that the Timberland style you purchase online matches a style that can be found on the official Timberland Web site. Many Timberland counterfeits have no corresponding authentic Timberland style.

UGG®

The maker of UGG® boots is unusual among shoe makers in providing information on how to avoid counterfeit products and actively encouraging its customers to fight counterfeiting. A quick visit to the counterfeit education section of the Web site www.uggaustralia.com could save you from wasting your money on a fake pair of UGG® boots.

Inside the Shoe:

❑ Does the label inside the boot read "Made in China"? (Note: Genuine UGG® boots are made in China by an American company called Deckers Inc. A "Made in New Zealand" label is actually a bad sign. The only exceptions are UGG® Nightfall, UGG® Sundance, and UGG® Ultra boots.)

❑ Is the label white? All genuine Decker's UGG® boots have white labels, never blue.

The Sole of the Shoe:

❑ Is there a registered trademark symbol (®) on the sole of the shoe? Fake UGG® boots usually have the brand name without the registered trademark symbol.

Additional Features:

❑ Do the boots feel like they are made from real sheepskin?

❑ **Tip:** If you rub synthetic wool, the hair will come out easily and start to disintegrate. Synthetic hair is also not as soft as real sheepskin.

❑ Do the boots smell like they are made from real sheepskin? Do not be afraid to use your nose to sniff out a fake! Be suspicious of any scent of glue or chemicals.

❑ Do your UGG® boots come with a cream-colored card describing how to care for your UGG® boots? These cream-colored cards replaced Care booklets shipped with UGG® boots made prior to June 2007.

Note: All "camel-colored" UGG® boots are fakes. Deckers Inc. does not make UGG® boots in that color.

Final Word

One of the best ways to spot counterfeits is to look for quality workmanship. Authentic designer shoes are made from the finest materials. Stitching and label attachment should be immaculate. Seams should be smooth with no traces of glue, cut-away leather, or unsightly wrinkles.

If a particular de-
signer brand is not listed
in the pages above, you
can visit the Web sites
www.portero.com   or
www.net-a-porter.com.
Both of these sites sell
authenticated designer
items. Even better, they
include excellent pic-
tures of designer shoes

taken from various angles. You can zoom into these pictures to examine
shoe details.

In addition to www.portero.com and www.net-a-porter.com,
designer shoes can be securely purchased from Saks Fifth Avenue, Bar-
neys New York, Neiman Marcus, and Bergdorf Goodman.

FUN FACTS ABOUT DESIGNER BRANDS

Armani

- The first Armani hotel is
  located on the first 34 floors
  of the Burj Khalifa, formerly
  known as the Burj Dubai, the
  tallest building in the world.
  Armani hotels have been
  planned for Milan, London,
  and New York.

- Armani was the first designer
  to ban models with a body
  mass index under 18 (equivalent to a size zero) after Uruguayan
  model Luisel Ramos dropped dead from heart failure related to
  anorexia.

Chanel

- Coco Chanel was friends with Picasso and Stravinsky. She had an
  affair with the Duke of Westminster (among other influential men),

but when asked why she never married, Chanel famously replied: "There have been several Duchesses of Westminster. There is only one Chanel."[8]

- Two biopics about Coco Chanel were released in 2009: *Coco avant Chanel* and *Coco Chanel & Igor Stravinsky*. Neither film mentions that Chanel collaborated with the Nazis during World War II.

Christian Dior

- Christian Dior's family made its fortune manufacturing fertilizer. Dior attended the *École des Sciences Politiques* to satisfy his parents' hopes that he would become a diplomat.

- As a young man, Dior sold sketches on the street for roughly 10 cents each.

Christian Louboutin

- Starting at age 12, Christian Louboutin used to sneak out of school to watch showgirls in Paris nightclubs. Showgirls were the inspiration behind his decision to become a shoe designer: "They influenced me a lot. If you like high heels, it's really the ultimate high heel—it's all about the legs, how they carry themselves, the embellishment of the body. They are the ultimate icons."[9]

- Louboutin has never owned a television and admits that he is "not very ambitious."[10]

- The 1987 German movie "Wings of Desire" inspired Louboutin to learn to swing on a trapeze; he installed a trapeze in his studio.

---

8 "High Priestess of High Fashion: GABRIELLE CHANEL" *Time*, August 22, 1960 (visited March 4, 2010); www.time.com/time/magazine/article/0,9171,869848,00.html.

9 Nina Jones, "Christian Louboutin: the sole man," *The Telegraph*, August 10, 2008 (visited March 4, 2010); www.telegraph.co.uk/fashion/3365106/Christian-Louboutin-the-sole-man.html.

10 *Id.*

Gucci

- Despite mythology about the Gucci family's having been saddle makers to wealthy Florentine families, Guccio Gucci left Italy to work as a dishwasher at the London Savoy after his father's hat-making business went under. He worked his way up to being a waiter while observing the habits of London's wealthiest citizens. Seeing their obsession with fancy leather luggage, Gucci eventually returned to Italy and learned the art of leatherwork.

- The compact AMC Hornet Sportabout station wagons were offered in Gucci models in 1972 and 1973.

Jimmy Choo

- Jimmy Choo was born in Malaysia to a family of shoemakers. He reportedly made his first pair of shoes when he was 11 years old.

- Jimmy Choo paid his way through the Cordwainers Technical College in London Borough (now part of the London College of Fashion) by working in restaurants and cleaning a shoe factory.

Prada

- Founder Mario Prada did not allow women to enter his leather goods business. Nevertheless, his granddaughter Miuccia Prada—who has a Ph.D. in political science and was a member of the Communist party—inherited the company from her mother in 1978 and greatly expanded upon its success.

Manolo Blahnik

- Manolo Blahnik grew up on a banana plantation in the Canary Islands.

- Manolo Blahnik shoes are referenced in several popular TV shows. They are a favorite of Carrie Bradshaw on *Sex and the City* and worn by Karen Walker on *Will and Grace*.

Nike

- The Nike "swoosh" was designed by Carolyn Davidson, a student at University of Portland. She was paid 35 dollars for her work by

Phil Knight, the founder and chairman of Nike. Knight made it up to Davidson in 1983 when he presented Davidson with stock in the company and a "swoosh" diamond ring.

- The Nike "swoosh" was designed to represent the wings of the Greek goddess Nike, the goddess of victory. Historically, the goddess Nike was invoked on the battlefield. She was a symbol of athletic strength, speed, and glory. But Nike was portrayed with wings not because she could fly as high as Michael Jordan or move as fast as Michael Johnson; the wings served as a reminder that victory is fleeting—a very un-Nike-like sentiment!

Timberland

- The Grammy Award-winning rapper, singer, and record-producer Timbaland adopted his stage name after Timberland boots became popular in hip-hop culture. His given name is Timothy Zachery Mosley.

- In the song, "Can I Get A…" Jay-Z references Timberland boots when he raps: "Cause from now on you can witness Jay the I-con! With hoodies and Timbs on."

UGG®

- Ugg is alleged to be a generic term used in Australia and New Zealand since at least the 1970s to describe sheepskin boots. The word has been the subject of an extended trademark dispute.

Versace

- The late Princess Diana was offered one million British pounds (about $1.5 million in 1996) to walk down the runway in Versace to celebrate her divorce from Prince Charles. She declined the offer.

- Gianni Versace was murdered outside his Miami home by a rampage killer. Versace was 50 years old.

CHAPTER 7

How to Care for Shoes

GOOD SHOES ARE EXPENSIVE BUT WORTH THE INVESTMENT. IN THIS section, you will learn ways to extend the life of your shoes by caring for them properly.

You will discover how to:

- properly clean and care for your athletic shoes
- clean, condition, polish, and waterproof your leather shoes
- remove scuff marks
- break-in a pair of stiff shoes

and much more! The goal is to keep your shoes looking and feeling great for longer—at last something that makes your feet *and* your wallet happy.

HOW TO CLEAN ATHLETIC SHOES

No matter how clean you keep your feet, athletic shoes start to smell after a while. And no wonder! With thousands of sweat glands, your feet are one of the sweatiest parts of your body. All this sweat attracts bacteria. When you get a whiff of a pungent pair of shoes, it is actually the bacteria's excrement you are smelling. If that doesn't convince you to clean your athletic shoes from time to time, then I don't know what will!

But before you jump the gun and throw your dirty sneakers into the washing machine, read the guidelines below. You will extend the life of your athletic shoes if you wash them by hand. A little extra effort helps your shoes go the distance.

What You Need:
Bucket, water, neutral cleaner, scrub brush or toothbrush, baking soda, and newspaper

What You Do:

- **Step 1.** Remove the laces and inserts. These will be cleaned separately from the main body of the shoe.

- **Step 2.** Throw your laces into the washing machine along with a load of laundry. (Note: This is the only part of the shoe you will wash in the washing machine!) You can wash your laces inside a mesh laundry bag (usually used for delicates), if you are worried about losing them in the wash. Pre-soak white laces in bleach if they are really dirty.

- **Step 3.** Allow your inserts to air out in a well-ventilated area. If they smell, sprinkle the inserts with baking soda.

- **Step 4.** Now it's time to turn your attention to your shoes. Fill a bucket with soapy water. Be sure to use a neutral soap. Liquid dish detergent works well, but you can also use a gentle all-purpose cleaner such as Simple Green®. Allow your shoes to soak to loosen any tough stains.

- **Step 5.** For this next step, you will need a scrub brush and some elbow grease. Clean the shoes inside and out. Feel free to dig into those tough stains, but don't scrub so hard that you ruin the fabric of the uppers. Use a toothbrush to tackle hard-to-reach stains in the shoes' grooves and creases.

- **Step 6.** Rinse the shoes thoroughly. Soap residue will stiffen the fabric of the shoes.

- **Step 7.** The way you dry your shoes is just as important as the way you wash them. NEVER PUT SHOES IN THE DRYER. The extreme heat can change the shoes' shape. Instead, allow your shoes to air dry. It helps to stuff newspaper inside the shoes to draw the moisture out.

Old tennis shoes or canvas sneakers can sometimes be tossed into the washing machine with a load of towels. But for athletic shoes, hand washing is the way to go. Extra care will pay off in the long run. Your shoes (and feet) will thank you!

ADDITIONAL CARE FOR ATHLETIC SHOES

In addition to regularly cleaning your athletic shoes, there are several steps you can take to extend their life.

- **Rotate your shoes regularly.** Rotating your shoes is important for two reasons: it allows the shoes to dry completely between work-outs, and it gives the foam in a shoe's sole time to decompress. (Every time you run or exercise, the supportive foam in your shoe's sole compresses. Athletic shoes go flat once compressed foam loses its ability to bounce back.)

  Rotating two identical pairs of shoes is an especially good idea if you have found a pair of shoes you really like. Most running shoe models are discontinued every 12-to-15 months. By purchasing two pairs at once, you extend the life of each pair *and* save yourself the hassle of trying out a new shoe. However, two pairs of shoes is only necessary if you run or workout more than four times a week.

- **Untie your laces *before* removing your shoes.** It is tempting to slip off athletic shoes without untying the laces, but this practice will gradually wear down the shoe's heel counter.

- **Use orthopedic inserts.** A great way to make old shoes feel like new is to replace the shoe's old insoles with new orthopedic insoles available at most shoe stores and pharmacies.

- **Sprinkle your shoes with baking soda to eliminate odor.** A little baking soda goes a long way when it comes to absorbing moisture and eliminating foot odor. If you prefer a more high-tech approach, you can purchase anti-fungal deodorizing foot sprays.

LEATHER SHOE CARE

The full spectrum of caring for your leather shoes includes cleaning, conditioning, polishing, and waterproofing. It may sound like a lot of work, but once the basic materials are gathered you will find that the occasional maintenance your leather shoes require is well worth it. With proper care you can extend the life of your leather shoes by years.

How to Clean Leather Shoes

Dust! Dust! Dust! Believe it or not, the most important thing you can do to preserve the life of your leather shoes is to keep them dust-free.

When small grains of dust are allowed to accumulate on leather shoes, they cut into the leather with every step you take.

You don't need anything special to wipe the dust off your leather shoes. Any dry or damp rag will do. Some people also like to use saddle soap or another moisturizing soap such as Dove. Apply the soap to the outside of the shoe. Be sure to wipe off the excess with a clean, dry cloth.

How to Condition Leather Shoes

Over time leather shoes lose some of the natural oils that make them soft and pliable. This is especially true of leather shoes that are stored in warm, dry climates, or leather shoes that are polished with wax.

Choose a conditioner that is specific to the type of leather used to make your shoes. Be careful not to apply *too* much conditioner; the conditioner should soak into the leather without leaving your shoes feeling greasy. Wipe away any excess.

Note: You do not need to use a leather shoe conditioner if you use a conditioning soap, or regularly apply a paste or cream polish to your shoes. These products already function as conditioners.

How to Polish Leather Shoes

When polishing leather shoes, you need to choose between four basic forms of shoe polish: cream, paste, wax, and liquid.

Most people recommend a cream or paste polish. These types of polishes perform wonders when it comes to concealing scratches or other blemishes in the leather. Cream and paste polishes soak into the leather, resulting in color that lasts. They also can act as conditioners.

If you don't want to use a cream or paste polish, you have two options:

Use Wax Polish

Use wax polish if your shoes are regularly exposed to the elements (rain, mud, etc.).

Pros: Wax polish offers extra protection for your shoes.
and a first-class shine.

Cons: Wax polish may dry out leather.

Use Liquid Polish
Use liquid polish if you want polish that will dry
quickly.

Pros: Liquid polish can be applied quickly.

Cons: Liquid polish comes in fewer colors than other
types of polish. It also does not last as long or cover im-
perfections as well as cream and paste polishes. Some
people even claim that liquid polish ruins leather.

What You Need:
Rag, soft-bristled shoe brush and your choice of shoe polish.

Note: Shoe polish can be applied either using a cloth or a brush. If
you decide to use a brush, make sure that the bristles are soft and will
not damage the leather. It is best to purchase a special "shoe shining"
brush.

    In order to polish your shoes properly, you will either need two
brushes and one rag, or two rags.

What You Do:
- **Step 1.** The first step is to choose a polish that matches the the color
  of your shoes. Be sure to try the polish on a discreet area of
  the shoe before brushing it across the entire leather upper.
- **Step 2.** Take the first brush or rag and dip it into the polish. Firmly
  brush or rub the polish across the shoe, being careful to
  work the polish into the shoe's crevices. Apply more polish
  as needed.
- **Step 3.** Once you have applied the polish, use a clean brush or rag
  to buff the shoe.

- **Step 4.** Step 4 is an optional step for those people who have decided to use brushes to polish their shoes. After buffing the polished shoe with a clean brush, give the shoe a final shine with a clean cloth.

Tip

Buffing your shoes with a clean brush or rag is absolutely essential; if you don't remove the excess polish you will wind up with pant cuffs dyed to match your shoes!

How to Waterproof Leather Shoes

After you have cleaned, conditioned and polished your shoes, there is only one step left: waterproofing.

You have two basic choices:

Use a Wax or Oil

Use wax or oil if your shoes are worn primarily outdoors (e.g., hiking boots), or if the shoe is made of a mixed material such as nylon and leather.

To Apply: Clean shoes first. Then apply the wax or oil with a cloth or brush. Be sure to work the product into the shoes' creases. Wipe away the excess, and allow the shoes to stand overnight.

Warning: Waterproofing oils and waxes should never be applied to suede or nubuck as they will damage the quality of the leather.

Use a Waterproofing Spray

Use a waterproofing spray if your shoes are made of a more delicate leather, or if your climate is only mild to moderately wet.

To Apply: Clean the shoes first. Hold the spray 6 inches away from the shoes and apply an even coat. Allow the shoes to stand overnight.

Make sure to choose a waterproofing spray designed for the specific material of your shoes. There are different sprays for leather, fabric, suede and nubuck.

Final word: Both methods have their advantages. Some waterproofing oils, such as mink oil, actually condition leather shoes. A waterproofing spray is without a doubt easier to apply. Ultimately, the decision comes down to the requirements of the specific leather used to make your shoes.

How to Store Leather Shoes

The way you store your leather shoes is just as important as the way you clean and condition them.

Shoe trees can help maintain the shape of leather shoes when you are not wearing them. They are available in plastic and wood. Plastic shoe trees are cheaper, but wooden ones (especially shoe trees made out of cedar) help to absorb moisture and eliminate shoe odor. As is true with athletic shoes, moisture shortens the lifespan of a pair of leather shoes. It causes the leather to decay, wrinkle and, of course, to smell.

There are two types of shoe trees: split and solid. Split shoe trees are best for shoes made out of soft leather. They are designed to fit a variety of shoe widths. Solid shoe trees work well for rigid leathers and shoes of average width.

The picture to the left is an example of a solid shoe tree. A shoe tree with a split toe would have, as its name suggests, a wooden toe that was split into two pieces. You can adjust the distance between the two pieces to accommodate a variety of shoe widths.

Shoe trees come in a variety of sizes and shapes for both men's and women's shoes. They range in price from 15-to-20 dollars, and most customers find them to be well worth the investment.

Caring for Special Types of Leather Shoes

OSTRICH	Ostrich leather is particularly coveted because it is extremely soft. This also means that ostrich leather is extremely delicate. It is *very* important to keep ostrich leather shoes dust-free. Use neutral leather cleaner and conditioning cream polish on a regular basis.
SNAKE, LIZARD, CROCODILE	Lizard, crocodile, and snake leathers are particularly dry. Regular application of a conditioning soap or polish is a must! Be careful that dust and conditioner residue do not collect between the scales.
SUEDE	Use a special suede brush and suede cleaner to clean suede shoes and restore the leather's nap. A less conventional cleaning technique involves rubbing cornmeal into the surface of the shoes, letting the shoes stand overnight and then brushing off the cornmeal in the morning.
NUBUCK	The general principle behind removing stains on nubuck shoes is to lightly sand the stain away. You can purchase a special nubuck eraser, or you can use items commonly found around the house such as medium-grade sand paper or a bath towel. Be sure to adjust the amount of force applied!
VITELLO, NAPA	These high-quality calfskin leathers should be cleaned and polished with soft cotton cloths rather than brushes.

Six Tried and Trusted Methods for Removing Scuff Marks

Few things are more irritating than splurging on a new pair of shoes only to have them marred by scuff marks a few days later. Luckily, most scuff marks are removed easily.

METHOD #1: TOOTHPASTE

Believe it or not, toothpaste (or a home-made paste of water and baking soda) can work wonders when it comes to removing scuff marks. Use an old toothbrush to apply the paste and lightly buff away the unsightly marks. This method should remove black scuff marks from white shoes as well as white or gray scuff marks from black or dark-colored shoes.

METHOD #2: NAIL POLISH REMOVER

Nail polish remover can work miracles on scuffed white shoes, but you should proceed carefully. Make sure that your nail polish remover is labeled "non-acetone" and be sure to test the solution on a small, discreet area of the shoe first. If the shoe seems to be fine, go ahead and dip a Q-tip or a cotton ball in the solution and carefully buff away scuff marks. Nail polish works best on black scuff marks; it is not recommended for shoes with a shiny finish.

METHOD #3: MR. CLEAN® MAGIC ERASER®

If nail polish remover does not work, you can try Mr. Clean® Magic Eraser®. This cleaning solution can be purchased at most drugstores. It is safe to use on leather, and it can remove pen marks and dirt build-up in addition to scuff marks.

METHOD #4: HAND SANITIZER

Hand sanitizer is recommended to remove white scuff marks from black dress shoes. The alcohol solution in the hand sanitizer is supposed to remove scuff marks without harming the shoe's shiny finish. This is one method you should try on a "test area" of the shoe first!

METHOD #5: LAVENDER OIL

For a more natural approach, apply lavender oil to scuff marks on black dress or leather shoes. This oil should remove white scuff marks and restore the shoe's original shiny finish. Aura Cacia® Lavender Essential Oil is highly recommended.

METHOD #6: PETROLEUM JELLY

If you are prepared to apply a little elbow grease, petroleum jelly (sometimes referred to by the brand name Vaseline®) can work wonders to remove scuff marks from leather shoes. Just put a dollop of petroleum jelly on a paper towel or rag and buff away. Unlike nail polish remover or hand sanitizer, there is no danger that petroleum jelly will remove the shoe's finish. It is a good place to start.

Note: No matter what method you use, it is better to test it out on a small section of the shoe in a discreet area. The last thing you want is for your shoes to have scuff marks *and* a ruined finish!

HOW TO SAFELY BREAK IN A PAIR OF SHOES

Whether you've purchased a pair of high heels or hiking boots, breaking in shoes can be a painful process. Unfortunately, there is no short-cut. The best way to break in stiff, stubborn shoes is simply to wear them.

That said, there is no need to take your new hiking boots on an 11-mile hike. Trying to do too much too soon in a pair of stiff shoes will leave you with little more than painful blisters and a lifelong distrust of your new fancy footwear. The key is to start slow. Here are three *pain-free* methods that can get you on your way:

Method #1: Movie Magic

Put on your new shoes and watch a movie. Simply wearing the shoes for sustained periods of time without walking in them will soften the shoes' material.

Method #2: Stairmaster

Wear your shoes every day for no more than to 15-to-30 minutes. Be sure to go up and down stairs, or do other activities that will force the shoes to bend and flex. The goal of this approach is to divide the break-in process into manageable and pain-free chunks. Take your shoes off *immediately* if you notice a hotspot.

Method #3: Wet and Stretch

Put on your shoes and then use a spray bottle to target tight areas. Wear your shoes until they dry; they should end up better suited to the shape of your foot. To make this method even more effective use a mixture of 1 part rubbing alcohol and 3 parts water. Be sure to test the solution on a discreet area of the shoe first.

CHAPTER 8

How to Repair Shoes

Forget taking your shoes to the cobbler! You can successfully perform basic shoe repairs at home. In this section you will learn how to save money and extend the life of your shoes with simple do-it-yourself repair techniques.

You will discover how to:

- resole a shoe and attach a new heel
- stretch leather shoes
- adjust boots to fit your calves
- change the fit of athletic shoes with custom lacing

and much more! These repair methods are straightforward and fast. You do not have to be a craft whiz or expert handyman.

HOW TO RESOLE A SHOE[11]

For some of us, shoes are sentimental possessions, and it is worth going the extra mile (and saving the extra dime) to make a simple shoe repair rather than looking for a replacement. One of the most common shoe repairs is resoling a shoe. Here is a brief summary of how you can perform this simple repair in the comfort of your home:

What You Need:
Shoe glue, replacement soles, razor, or utility knife, file.

Note: Choose half-soles for shoes with elevated heels and full-soles for shoes with a flat sole. You can also purchase foam material and make your own replacement soles.

What You Do:

- Step 1. Clean the old soles of your shoes. Remove all gunk, grime, and dirt. If you clean the soles with water, allow them to dry completely before you continue with the repair.

- Step 2. Use a razor or utility knife to cut away the old soles.

- Step 3. Use the file (or sandpaper) to scuff the surface of the shoe where the sole was removed and the surface of the replacement sole that will be attached to the scuffed surface of the shoe. This creates rough surfaces that will help the new sole adhere to the shoe.

- Step 4. This next step depends on the type of soles you purchased. Self-adhering soles can be carefully aligned with the bottom of the shoe and then attached. Soles that are not self-adhering will require some kind of shoe-repair contact cement.

---

11 Many shoes have molded unitary outsoles made of synthetic material and bonded to the uppers. It is often impractical to replace the soles of such shoes. In any event, resoling such shoes is best left to professional cobblers. The described methods for replacing soles and heels are for shoes made by the traditional method of gluing, sewing, and nailing pieces of rubber and leather.

You should be able to find an appropriate product at your local shoe or hardware store.

- Step 5. The best way to reinforce the bond between the new soles and the old shoes is to walk around the house in them for several minutes.

- Step 6. Once the soles are firmly attached, use the utility knife to trim excess glue and leather. Use the file on the edges to give your new soles a smooth finish.

If your shoes also need a pair of new heels, then you will need to attach half-soles and replace the heel separately. Please read ahead to learn how to equip your old shoes with new heels.

HOW TO REPLACE A SHOE'S HEEL

A shoe's heel is often the first part of the shoe to need replacing. Look for heel tips or caps for women's shoes online or at your local shoe store. NewHeelTips.com carries heel tips in a wide range of sizes and shapes. The Web site has printable templates that allow you to determine the size and shape to order based on your worn-out heel tips, and illustrated instructions for removal of your old heel tips and installation of the new.

These replacement heel tips come with a screw or nail already inserted. The only tool required for the job is a pair of pliers to remove the old heel tips. The nails of the new heel tips are inserted into the heels and are secured to the shoe by tapping them against a hard surface.

For men's shoes, you may use the following procedure to replace the heels:

What You Need:
Shoe glue, replacement heels, file, shoe nails or screws, and a hammer or screwdriver

What You Do:

- Step 1. Remove any nails or screws that are used to keep the old heel in place. The old heel should come off with a few forceful tugs. Do not worry if you break the old heel in the process of removing it.

- Step 2. Use the file (or sandpaper) to scuff the area of the shoe where the new heel will be attached and the surface of the replacement heel that will butt against that area of the shoe. This is your chance to remove any glue or gunk and to repair the leather.

- Step 3. Apply shoe-repair contact cement to the area on the shoe where you will attach the heel. Carefully line up the replacement heel. Press the heel firmly to the shoe.

- Step 4. Once the glue has dried, reinforce the new heel with several nails or screws. Use the old heel as your guide. Be careful not to apply nails or screws too close to the edge of the heel as this will weaken the heel and make it more likely to break.

- Step 5. Use a file to remove any rough edges or glue residue.

HOW TO STRETCH LEATHER SHOES

Method #1 (For REALLY cool shoes)
Use this creative method to stretch leather shoes

What You Need:
Two Ziploc® (or similar) bags, water, and a freezer

What You Do:

- Step 1. Fill each Ziploc® bag 1/3 full of water. Be sure to seal the bags completely!

- Step 2. Place each bag in the area of the shoe you want to stretch. Most often this is the forefront of the shoe, or the toe-box. You will want to make sure that the bag fills up all excess space. Add more water, if necessary. If the shoe has an open toe, pull the bag slightly through the toe so that it pokes out the other side.

- Step 3. Put your shoes in the freezer.

- Step 4. Allow the water to freeze completely so that each bag is full of ice. Water, as you may remember from your elementary school science class, expands when frozen. The expansion of the water molecules will permanently stretch the leather of your shoes.

- Step 5. Once the bags are frozen solid, remove the shoes from the freezer and let them thaw for 20 minutes. Wipe off excess water, and try the shoes on for size. This method of stretching should be able to increase shoe size by a half to a full size.

Method #2
This method results in minimal stretching, but, unlike the ice method, it offers a custom fit.

What You Need:
Rubbing alcohol, water, and a spray bottle

What You Do:
- Step 1. Mix 1 part isopropyl rubbing alcohol with 3 parts water. Pour this mixture into a spray bottle.
- Step 2. Test this mixture on a small, discreet area of the shoe. Allow it to dry. Only continue to Step 3 if the mixture does *not* alter the shoe's finish.

- Step 3. Put on your shoes. Spray the mixture on areas of the shoe that feel tight.
- Step 4. Continue to wear the shoes until they are completely dry.

Tip

These methods works best on real leather shoes. Plastic or faux leather shoes may shrink back to their original size.

No matter which approach you take, it is a good idea to treat your shoes first with a leather moisturizer. If the leather is extra soft and supple, it will not crack when stretched. Feel free to use a simple conditioner such as petroleum jelly or saddle soap. Professional cobblers use a "shoe stretching" spray before stretching leather shoes. You can purchase such a product online or in most up-market shoe stores.

HOW TO SHORTEN HIGH HEELS

We all know that high heels are bad for our feet, ankles, knees, and posture. The list goes on! But that does not seem to stop us from wearing them. Pain may equal beauty in the short term, but at what price?

The good news is that lowering a heel by something even as subtle as 1/4 inch can relieve a tremendous amount of pressure on our feet, ankles, and knees. But alterations must be done carefully. If you lower the heel too much, you could distort the balance of the shoe. (Imagine a high heel shoe without its heel. The toe would point straight up into the air. At best, the shoe would be extremely uncomfortable. At worst, the shank would snap in two as soon as you put any weight on it.)

The Table Test

Here is an easy way of judging how much height a cobbler can take off a heel without distorting the shoe's fit. Take your high heeled shoe or boot and place it on the end of a table so that the heel hangs off. Be sure to keep the shoe level. Slowly lower the heel until the back end of the ball of the foot rests on the table. Whatever part of the heel hangs below table-level is expendable.

Be warned: It is rarely possible to shorten a heel by more than an inch, and even this reduction is too much in some cases. A 3-inch stiletto cannot magically transform into a flat.

A confident craftsperson could attempt to saw off the excess height and then attach a heel following the procedure found on page 117 However, this repair is best performed by an expert. Visit your friendly cobbler or shoe salesman for more information.

HOW TO ADJUST BOOTS TO FIT YOUR CALVES

There are few things more disappointing than finding a pair of stylish boots that fit your feet perfectly but not your calves. Unfortunately, altering these boots can be costly. Before paying a cobbler to fix boots that cost you a pretty penny in the first place, consider these alternatives.

- **Be Style Smart.** Look for boots with straps, laces or buckles that allow you to cinch or loosen the leather for a fit that is perfectly suited to your body. Ruched boots (think: gathered leather) offer a flexible fit. For shoppers with skinny legs, these boots fit loosely without looking like your leg is drowning in leather. For shoppers with more shapely calves, ruched boots give you a little extra wiggle room.

- **Buy Boots That Will Stretch**. Look for boots made out of soft, stretchable leather. Sometimes a tight boot will loosen after a few wears. You can also purchase leather-stretching spray at most shoe stores, or check out creative ways to stretch leather shoes on page 118 of this chapter.

- **Modify Your Wardrobe.** If you fall in love with a pair of boots that are too big around your calves, consider wearing them over pants or with thick socks. Tight boots can be worn with dresses and sheer nylons.

When all else fails, it is time for a visit to your friendly neighborhood cobbler. Cobblers can make tight boots bigger by adding elastic gussets. It is a little trickier to take-in big boots. The possibility of such an alteration will depend entirely on the way the boots are made. Ask your cobbler for details.

Be sure to tell the cobbler exactly how you intend to wear the boots to ensure a precise, custom fit! Don't have the boot altered to fit your bare leg if you plan to wear the boot with jeans.

SNAPSHOT: SHOE GOO®

Shoe Goo® is an industrial strength urethane rubber cement[12] that may be exactly what you are looking for when it comes to repairing your old shoes.

History
Invented in 1972, Shoe Goo® was originally designed to combat a problem known as "tennis toe." The clear gummy glue was applied to the toes of tennis shoes that had been worn down by dragging the shoes across the tennis court.

What Can You Do with Shoe Goo®? **Repairs in 5 minutes or less!**
Repair a Hole in the Sole of Your Shoe!

- Step 1. Remove the shoe's insole.

- Step 2. Use a piece of duct tape to cover the hole from the inside. This tape will prevent Shoe Goo® from forming a bump on the inside of your shoe as the glue dries.

- Step 3. Apply Shoe Goo® to the outside of the shoe. Use enough glue so that the hole is completely filled.

- Step 4. Allow the glue to dry 24 hours before wearing the shoe. Be sure to take the tape off in under 2 hours or it may become a permanent feature of the shoe!

---

12 FreeSole® Urethane Formula Shoe Repair is similar to Shoe Goo® and may be used instead.

Repair a rip in the fabric of your shoe!

- Step 1. Apply Shoe Goo® to both sides of the tear.

- Step 2. Wait several moments until the glue becomes tacky, and then firmly press the two ends in place.

- Step 3. Hold the ends in place for several minutes.

- Step 4. Allow the glue to dry. Apply another coat of Shoe Goo®, if necessary.

Re-finish a worn-down section of your shoe!

- Step 1. Coat the shoe in a thin layer of adhesive.

- Step 2. Allow the layer to dry before applying successive layers.

HOW TO REPAIR THE HEEL ON AN ATHLETIC SHOE

As any runner will tell you, most running shoes wear quickly and unevenly. This means that although your high-tech EVA midsole may have plenty of bounce left in it, the traction on the outer sole may have worn away. Or vice versa. One of the most common places running shoes wear down is on the inside of the shoe's heel. The fabric of the shoe wears away so that the plastic heel counter is exposed.

There are several ways to patch up this problem, each requiring varying levels of expertise and maintenance.

Method #1: The Quick Fix

The easiest way to fix an exposed heel counter is to slap a piece of duct tape over the tear in the fabric. The tape should last for several runs and can be replaced easily.

Method #2: The Do-It-Yourself Cobbler

The more labor-intensive approach is to use a piece of cloth. Look for material that is slippery yet durable. You want a fabric that will move with the motion of your heel. Nylon is a good choice, but be careful that the glue does not soak through the nylon and make the fabric hard. Other recommendations include denim, leather, and suede.

Tip

Look for an old jacket at a thrift store and use the leather elbow patches to reline the back of your shoe.

Once you have chosen your fabric, you are ready to patch your shoe.

- Step 1. Cut out a patch that is substantially larger than the size of the hole.
- Step 2. Remove the shoe's insole
- Step 3. Use a strong but flexible glue (Shoe Goo® or Gorilla Super Glue®[13]) to glue the patch in place.
- Step 4. If you are feeling ambitious, stitch the patch to the shoe. Stitching *and* gluing the patch will make the patch last longer.
- Step 5. Replace the shoe's insole.

LOOP IT, SWOOP IT, AND PULL!

Shoe tying may seem like elementary stuff. But believe it or not, you can put your shoe tying skills to serious work. With a little ingenuity, the fit of athletic shoes can be modified simply by adjusting the way you tie your laces.

For more information about fun shoe tying methods, check out Ian Fieggen's book *Laces* or his shoelace site at www.fieggen.com/shoelace.[14]

If your heel is slipping...

Try tying your laces in a "lace lock." This will allow you to tighten the laces around the ankle, which will help to secure your heel.

- Step 1. Lace your shoes normally, leaving the eyelet closest to the ankle open.
- Step 2. Take the *right* tail and thread it through the *right* eyelet so that the lace moves from the outside of the shoe to the inside. Do

---

13 Gorilla Super Glue® is a cyanoacrylate glue mixed with tiny rubber particles to add flexibility. Any cyanocrylate glue should be used with extreme caution because it instantly bonds to the skin.

14 Illustrations Copyright © 2003-2009 by Ian Fieggen; used with permission.

the same on the left side. Do not pull the lace all the way through! You want to create a loop just big enough for your little finger.

- Step 3. Once you have your two loops, take the laces and cross them. Now thread the tails through the two loops you created. Thread the *left* tail through the right loop, and the *right* tail through the left loop.

- Step 4. You are now ready to tie a normal bow. You should be able to tighten the laces at the ankle without tightening the entire shoe.

If your foot is narrow…

You can also use the lace lock to tighten the forefoot of your athletic shoes. This is particularly helpful for people with narrow feet.

- Step 1. Start to lace your shoes normally. Stop as soon as you complete the "X" through the second eyelet. This is where you will apply the lace lock.

- Step 2. Take the tail of the lace that extends from the second eyelet on the *right* side of the shoe and thread it through the third eyelet on the *right* side of the shoe. Do the same on the left side. Don't pull the laces all the way through! Make two small loops.

- Step 3. Once you have your two loops, cross the laces. Thread the left tail through the right loop and the right tail through the left loop. You've now created a lace

lock that will enable you to cinch your shoe tightly at the fore-front of your foot.

- Step 4. Continue lacing as normal. If your feet are extremely narrow, you can use an additional lace lock at the ankle.

If your shoe feels too tight...

People with wide feet or high arches sometimes find athletic shoes to be too constricting. Solve this problem by using a parallel lacing technique.

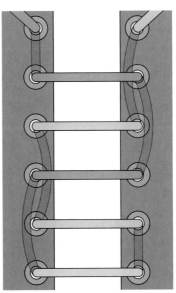

- Step 1. To make this explanation clearer, let's imagine that we are lacing the *right* shoe. Start by threading the lace through the first and second eyelets on the *left* side of the shoe. (This is the big toe side of the shoe.) The two tails should end up dangling *outside* the shoe.

- Step 2. Take the upper tail and cross to the *right* side of the shoe. Thread the lace through the first eyelet on the *right* side. The lace should move from the outside of the shoe to the inside of the shoe.

- Step 3. Thread this same tail through the *third* eyelet on the *right* side. (Notice we skipped one eyelet!) The lace should move from the inside of the shoe to the outside of the shoe.

- Step 4. Repeat this pattern using the same tail. (Thread the lace through the eyelet directly across the tongue. Then thread the lace through the eyelet on the same side, skipping one eyelet.)

- Step 5. Once you have reached the tongue, repeat the procedure with the other tail.

If your shoe is putting pressure on your big toe...

Often athletic shoes put unwanted pressure on the big toe. This can cause capillaries behind the toenail to burst, resulting in what is commonly referred to as a "black toenail." To address this problem, use a lacing technique that enables you to pull the fabric of the upper away from the big toe.

- Step 1. Thread the lace through the eyelet closest to the big toe.

- Step 2. Take the inside end of the lace and thread it through the eyelet furthest away from the big toe. This will be the eyelet on the opposite side of the shoe closest to the ankle.

- Step 3. Pull the lace so that the majority of the slack is up by the big toe. (The lace near the ankle only needs to be long enough to tie a bow.)

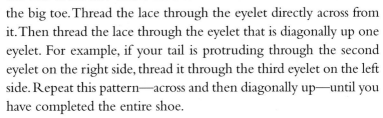

- Step 4. Lace the entire shoe using the end of the lace that is next to the big toe. Thread the lace through the eyelet directly across from it. Then thread the lace through the eyelet that is diagonally up one eyelet. For example, if your tail is protruding through the second eyelet on the right side, thread it through the third eyelet on the left side. Repeat this pattern—across and then diagonally up—until you have completed the entire shoe.

- Step 5. Before tying the bow, tug on the lace that is opposite from the big toe (i.e., the tail that you did *not* lace the shoe with). You should be able to lift the fabric of the upper off of the toe, relieving the pressure.

If your toes feel cramped...

If your shoes only feel tight around the toes, lace your shoes with two laces that are shorter than the normal length.[15]

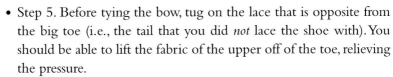

---

15 The length depends on the number of pairs of eyelets engaged by the laces, and the distance between eyelets both across the shoe and vertically.

- Step 1. Using the first lace, lace the first three eyelets as you normally would and tie a bow.
- Step 2. With the second lace, lace up the rest of the shoe and tie a second bow. This technique allows you to tie a loose bow near the toes while maintaining a tight fit around the ankle.

Note: A less esthetically pleasing solution may be to eliminate the lower lace entirely, only lacing the upper eyelets.

If the shoe rubs the top of your foot...

Sometimes the fabric of the upper can rub the top of your foot raw. If you are suffering from this problem, try this simple technique.

- Step 1. Lace your shoe normally, but skip the eyelets in the area where your foot is most sore. Without laces cinched over the sore area, irritation should decrease.

Note: You should be able to skip a couple of eyelets without compromising the fit of your shoes. For best results, do not skip two eyelets in a row.

CHAPTER 9

What to Do with Old Shoes

WHILE SHOES MAY NOT BE THE FIRST THING THAT COME TO MIND WHEN you hear the word "recycling," there are plenty of ways to find a new home or purpose for an old, unwanted shoe.

In this chapter you will learn about various ways to give old shoes new life. You will discover:

- what happens to shoes that are not sold at thrift shops
- how old athletic shoes are turned into new athletic surfaces
- how to donate shoes to disaster relief efforts
- where to buy shoes made from recycled materials

and much more! By the end of the chapter, you will discover new possibilities for the old shoes buried in the back of your closet.

SNAPSHOT: SOLES 4 SOULS—DONATING OLD SHOES TO A GOOD CAUSE

Soles 4 Souls is a non-profit organization that collects donations of new and gently worn shoes and distributes them to people in need in the United States and abroad. Soles 4 Souls specializes in disaster relief efforts. In fact, the organization was founded after the CEO of Soles 4 Souls, Wayne Elsey, privately decided to collect footwear donations for the victims of the 2004 tsunami in Southeast Asia.

Domestic Donations

Soles 4 Souls donates shoes to summer camps for abused or neglected youth, shelters for women who are victims of domestic violence, and inner city hospitals. The organization also distributes shoes to people who live in the Appalachian Mountain Region and on Navajo and Hopi reservations. Soles 4 Souls also donated shoes to people in need after Hurricane Katrina.

International Donations

Soles 4 Souls provides shoes for vulnerable populations abroad such as orphans, village women and people who work in landfills.

Contact

To learn more about the people and organizations Soles 4 Souls supports, visit the organization's Web site at www.soles4souls.org.

You can also contact the organization directly by phone at (615) 391-5723; (866) 521-SHOE; or by e-mail at info@giveshoes.org.

For up to date warehouse locations and shipping addresses, visit www.soles4souls.org/about/shipping.html.

SNAPSHOT: NIKE'S REUSE-A-SHOE PROGRAM— RECYCLING OLD RUNNING SHOES

Serious runners may need a new pair of running shoes every 3 months. This high turnover rate means that a lot of athletic shoes end up in garbage cans, and ultimately, our nation's landfills. Recycling these shoes is one way to reduce waste.

Nike's Reuse-A-Shoe recycling program started in the 1990s in an attempt to rectify this situation. Nike's goal: to turn old tennis shoes into brand spanking new athletic surfaces and playground equipment!

WHAT | *kinds of shoes does Nike accept?*

The Reuse-A-Shoe Program accepts shoes from any brand, not just Nike. It is important, however, that the shoes are clean and that they do not have any metal cleats. Nike does not currently recycle dress shoes or flip-flops.

WHERE | *can I donate my old shoes?*

Nike has placed Reuse-A-Shoe bins in 300 locations across the United States as well as in drop-off locations in Australia, New Zealand, and Western Europe.

If you do not live near a drop-off location, you can ship your old athletic shoes to the Nike processing center in Wilsonville, Oregon.

Nike Recycling Center c/o Reuse-A-Shoe
26755 SW 95th Ave.
Wilsonville, OR 97070

Visit the Web site www.nikereuseashoe.com before shipping your shoes to make sure that the URL is current. You can also contact the Nike Reuse-A-Shoe program by sending them an e-mail. Visit www.nikereuseashoe.com/contact-us to send your message.

Note: Consider the energy and money required to ship your shoes. It may actually be "greener" and more economical to donate your old shoes locally or to find a creative use for them at home.

HOW | *does the recycling process work?*

Once enough shoes have been collected at a drop-off location, they are shipped in bulk to one of Nike's Reuse-A-Shoe processing centers located in Wilsonville, Oregon and Meerhout, Belgium. Here, each shoe is divided into three sections: the rubber outsole, the foam midsole, and the fabric upper. Each section of the shoe is ground up into raw material that is collectively referred to as "Nike Grind" and used to manufacture new products.

- **THE RUBBER OUT-SOLE** is used to make playground surfaces, running tracks as well as outsoles for new shoes.

- **THE FOAM MIDSOLE** is transformed into cushioning material for outdoor tennis courts and basketball courts.

- **THE FABRIC UPPER** is used to create pads placed beneath indoor volleyball courts and basketball courts.

For more information about how to donate shoes, or to learn how to apply to run a Nike Reuse-A-Shoe shoe drive, visit Nike's Reuse-A-Shoe Web site at www.nikereuseashoe.com.

DONATING SHOES DOMESTICALLY

The following list is a sampling of shoe-recycling programs or goodwill organizations that accept shoe donations. You may use it to generate ideas about how to donate shoes at a local or national level.

Planet Aid, Inc.

Planet Aid, Inc. collects shoes in the United States from 19 states and attempts to resell them. Not only do these shoes find new homes, but the proceeds from the sale are used to finance education, community development, and HIV/AIDs programs in Asia and Africa.

Check out the Planet Aid, Inc. Web site at www.planetaid.org to see if your state is listed.

The Shoe Bank

This organization was established to collect gently worn shoes for the homeless population in Dallas, Texas. Today it provides more than 20,000 people with proper footwear—at home and abroad.

Shoes are collected at 160 elementary schools in Texas. E-mail Mike Barringer at MichaelBarringer@sbcglobal.net to learn about drop-off locations near you.

The Little Rock Roadrunners Club in Arkansas

Shoes collected by the Little Rock Roadrunners Club are donated to people in need in the Little Rock community. Adult shoes are used to provide footwear for the homeless population and children's shoes are given to children in need of proper footwear in local schools.

Search the web to see if your community has a runners club with a shoe donation program or suggest that your local runners club start one!

Northern Cook County Shoe Recycling Program in Illinois

This recycling program collects athletic shoes and sends them to recycling plants where they are remade into athletic surfaces.

Ask your local recycling program if there are any shoe-recycling centers near you.

Note: Do not forget about your local Good Will or Salvation Army.

DONATING SHOES INTERNATIONALLY

The following list includes organizations that collect shoes primarily for people in need abroad.

Heart and Sole

The Michigan State University College of Osteopathic Medicine collects shoes for some of the world's poorest people.

Visit www.com.msu.edu/pub-rel/heartandsole/ to learn about the recipients of Heart and Sole's shoe donation program.

Hope Runs

Hope Runs is a non-profit NGO that operates in Kenya and Tanzania. The organization accepts donations of used and new running shoes. These shoes are given to children orphaned as a result of AIDS and other orphaned or abandoned children in Kenya and Tanzania who learn about personal health and social entrepreneurship through running. Hope Runs also accepts donations of other athletic equipment and is interested in forging connections with international running groups and marathoners.

Visit www.hoperuns.org for more details about where and how to send your donations.

One World Running

Previously known as "Shoes for Africa," One World Running is a non-profit organization based in Boulder, Colorado. It sends donated athletic shoes to African national athletic teams.

To read more about the project, visit One World Running's blog at www.oneworldrunning.blogspot.com.

Samaritan's Shoe Relief Mission

The "Shoes of Hope" project aims to collect 10 million shoes for 10 million impoverished children over the next 10 years.

Learn how to host a shoe drive or make a donation at www.samaritansfeet.org/our-programs.

Shoe4Africa

This organization is based in New York City and donates shoes to athletes in Africa. It is also collecting donations for the only public children's hospital in sub-Saharan Africa.

Find out how to donate at www.shoe4africa.org or e-mail info@ shoe4africa.org for more information.

Shoe Recycle Program Team Barrios, Mexico

This program collects donated shoes and gives them to underprivileged citizens in Mexico.

The organization has no Web site, but you can find out more by writing to 16199 East 48th Avenue #2521, Denver, Colorado 80239.

Note: Some of the organizations listed above have boxes of donated shoes that cannot be shipped abroad because the organizations cannot afford to pay the international shipping fees. Consider making a cash donation in addition to or instead of donating your shoes.

CREDENTIAL CLOTHING

WHEN OLD SHOES TAKE A TRIP AROUND THE WORLD

Any regular thrift store shopper knows that some used shoes and shirts just do not sell. So what happens to these double cast-offs? If their owners put them up for sale and no one bites, is it worth keeping them around? The answer to that question—if you are at all concerned about limiting our nation's ever-growing landfills—is an unequivocal yes.

Many thrift stores sort and bundle their unsold merchandise and ship it overseas where these soft goods will hopefully find an owner. This unsold merchandise is called "credential clothing."

Credential clothing is sold by weight. A typical rate ranges from 37 to 55 cents per pound. Pairs of shoes are bound together and then packed in Gaylord boxes (pallet-sized boxes made of corrugated fiberboard) or poly-fiber bags. A typical Gaylord box of shoes weighs 650 pounds. A trailer loaded to capacity with Gaylord boxes full of shoes weighs approximately 42,000 pounds.

So what happens to these un- wanted shoes once they reach their final destination?

Some unsold footwear is profit- able in the foreign market. It is not uncommon for 50 pounds bags of shoes to be purchased by an overseas merchant and then sold in an open-air market.

Credential clothing is also sent to disaster relief areas, purchased by thrift stores in the United States, and recycled for base materials such as cotton, wool, and rubber.

CREATIVE WAYS TO RECYCLE YOUR SHOES

Turn Running Shoes into Gardening Shoes

If your shoes are shot, consider transforming a pair of first-rate running shoes into a pair of gardening shoes. Or work shoes. Or shoes that you wear when you paint the house. Some athletes like to wear their running shoes until they are just about flat, and then put them aside to use when they are running cross-country on muddy trails.

Make Shoe Art

If your old shoes are actually "old" (i.e., they are your Great Aunt Bertha's 1930s pumps), you might be able to sell them to a thrift shop for a pretty penny. For those of you who are more sentimental, consider displaying your old shoes as a piece of art. The right pair of shoes can look beautiful hanging on a wall or displayed in a shadow box. They may be the perfect decoration for a young girl's bedroom, or function as a special keepsake to remind of a special event such as a wedding or baptism.

Give the Shoe to Fido

Chances are your dog has been waiting to get his teeth on your sweaty shoes since the day you bought them. Well, now is his chance! Old shoes make the perfect "toy" for dogs that love to gnaw on just about anything. Remember to remove the laces before you turn the shoes over to your pup!

Let Your Children Play Dress Up

Give unwanted shoes to your children to play dress-up. Your child will get far more pleasure out of prancing around in an out-of-style high heel shoe than you will get from staring at that ugly thing every time you open your closet.

PURCHASING SHOES MADE FROM RECYCLED MATERIALS

In addition to recycling your old shoes, you can purchase new shoes made out of recycled materials. Here is a quick look at some standout recycled footwear companies:

Worn Again | www.wornagain.co.uk
Materials: Parachutes, prison blankets, car seats, scrap leather
Claim to Fame: Shoes made from 99 percent recycled materials

Jade Planet | www.jadeplanet.net
Materials: Soda pop bottles, cushioning from car seats and tire rubber
Claim to Fame: 100% vegan products

Simple Shoes | www.simpleshoes.com
Materials: Silk, bamboo, organic cotton, recycled inner tubes and paper
Claim to Fame: Simple designs made sustainably

Splaff Flops | www.splaff.com
Materials: Race car tires, bicycle inner tube straps, hemp
Claim to Fame: Recycled sandals with a 6-month guarantee

Patagonia | www.patagonia.com/shoes
Materials: Recycled EVA, cork, latex from Hevea trees
Claim to Fame: Quality shoes, eco-friendly
Also, be sure to check out: Vegan Essentials, Planet Shoes, Teva Curbside Collection, and TOMS Shoes.

Index